Zenna Dare

Zenna Dare

Copyright © Rosanne Hawke 2014

Published by Rhiza Press

www.rhizapress.com.au

PO Box 1519, Capalaba Qld 4157

First Edition published by Lothian, 2002.

ISBN 0 7344 0356 9

Second Edition published by Rhiza Press, 2014.

ISBN 978 1 925139 03 7

National Library of Australia Cataloguing-in-Publication entry :

Author: Hawke, Rosanne, author.

Title: Zenna dare / Rosanne Hawke.

ISBN: 9781925139037 (paperback)

Target Audience: For young adults.

Subjects: Families--Fiction.

          Reconciliation--Fiction.

Dewey Number: A823.3

ZENNA DARE

ROSANNE HAWKE

rhiza press

Acknowledgements

I wish to thank the Government of South Australia for providing a grant through ARTSA which enabled me to research and write *Zenna Dare*; also the Eleanor Dark Foundation for a residency at Varuna, The Writers' House where *Zenna Dare* was completed.

The beginning quote from the CD album *Acres of Blue* is used with kind permission of Jeanette Wormald. Also verses from the Cornish folksongs, 'Lamorna' and 'The White Rose' have been used with the permission of Mike O'Connor OBE from the book, *This Song I'll Sing to You: Songs the Cornish Love to Sing*, edited by Mike O'Connor, Lyngham House, 1998.

The writing of *Zenna Dare* would not have been possible without the following people, whose help is greatly appreciated: students of Kapunda High School class of 2000 — Jayan Mace, Hannah Thomas, Shari Wilson, Lisa Solomon, Paula Kernich, Tara Jones and Kristy Ashton; Paul McCarthy and library staff at Kapunda High; Janet Fletcher; Leanne Gates; my editor, Gwenda Smyth; Dr Virginia Lowe; Fred Warrior, Chairperson of the Ngadjuri People's Council; Fran Knight; Sue Anderson; Ruth and Howie Sumner; Jacinta Warren; David Kilpin; Dr John Foster; Janet Williams; Peter Galliford; Lilian James (Ula Ruthvelen, Bard of Cornwall); Mr Hampel and Mark of Kapunda Camel Farm; Gill and Hans Albers of Anlaby Station;

Kapunda Council, Library and Museum staff; Laura of Laura's Collectables; Mortlock Library staff, Adelaide; Cornish Studies Library at Redruth; The Courtney Library; Royal Institution of Cornwall, Truro (accessed via the Web); Jill and Peter Billings (our long-lost Cornish cousins); Papa who provided the music, and Pawley White (Gunwyn, Former Grand Bard of Cornwall) for his wonderful old-world hospitality and the use of his private library in Camborne, Cornwall.

FOR JENNIFER, WHO FIRST TOLD ME STORIES

Being Australian isn't about how long you've
lived here or what you or your parents look like;
it's about a sense of belonging to the land.

Jeanette Wormald

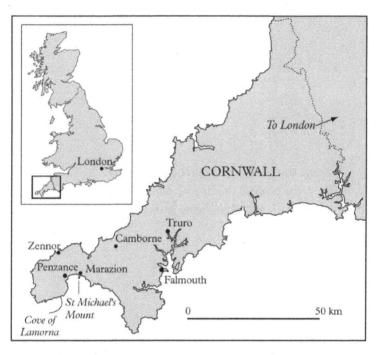

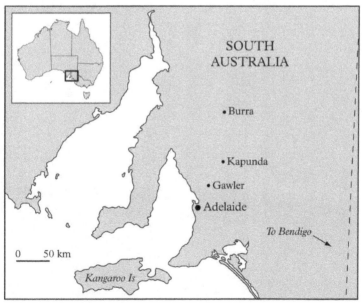

PRELUDE

Before the last strains from the orchestra had faded, the uproar began: clapping, stamping. Men were standing, shouting, 'Bravo! Encore!' The boy bringing the silk flowers from offstage paused behind the curtain. The orchestra leader rose, lifted his violin into position. Zenna watched the audience through a mist of tears and shock. Only later would it turn to a surprised and fearful happiness. So it had come to this. She had taken Drury Lane by storm.

The young queen sat in her box, smiling, nodding at the lead violinist. Balfe's overture began again and Zenna was handed the lute. She tossed her dark curls back, turned once, twice; waited for her cue, as the gypsy skirt swished against her ankles. Then she began to sing. The hall fell quiet and all was forgotten: the griefs and fears, the drudgery at home that only drink and song could relieve. All that mattered was the beautiful forest girl, Arline, singing her love for a gypsy prince.

Zenna sang, and that night she conquered much more than a prince in a play.

JT

THE LIBRETTO

JENEFER

Imagine if I had a terminal illness. One where I was on a life-support system. Drips changed every hour. Write-ups in the paper about how brave I was, how the family was proud of me for hanging on. Dad would want the best for me. Asking what I needed next. And I wouldn't have to move away. Incredible. Uprooting someone at the beginning of Year 12. He wouldn't do it if I had leukemia. People choose to move from the country to the city. I can understand that when a small school doesn't have a senior high section. But the other way round? We're moving to some tiny place of historical interest near the Barossa Valley. Nothing I can do about it. This is it! My life is about to be ruined and my father needs a psychologist.

So old Aunt Dorie wanted to move into a home. Do we have to take up residence in the family house? Oh no, I said. Oh yes, said Dad. He even sent CVs and got a transfer to the uni campus at Roseworthy. Once that came through there was no stopping the wheels of fate. Steffi just acts as if she's supporting a losing footy team, as though she can't stop now, not after twelve years of being a fan, whether she agrees with their methods or not.

'See where they grow all the wheat, kids?' Dad's

checking on us in the rear-vision mirror. Paddocks are so boring this time of year — a hot-looking, faded yellow, with equally faded purple hills behind. Can't think what Dad's so excited about. The view out the window looks like a postcard that's been left in a deli window for twenty years. At least the twin-cab is air-conditioned. The weather is positively evil out there.

Hamilton and Kate don't even look. They're sharing the Cheezels. That's not strictly correct — Kate's bestowing a few upon Hamilton. And the few Hamilton gets he's sharing with Sher Khan on his lap. For once Sher Khan is acting like his name, scoffing down the Cheezels and squeezing his whiskery grey nose against Hamilton's hand, sniffing for more. Don't know how many times I told Hamilton Sher Khan was not a good name for a rabbit, and a dwarf one at that. But Hamilton was adamant. He has a quiet way of doing that sometimes. Living with Kate has a lot to do with how Hamilton is.

It was Rudyard Kipling. Hamilton has this little book of animal stories about how certain ones got their tails and spots. 'How do you know he hasn't got a tiger heart?' Hamilton said that day. I wonder if Hamilton wishes he was a tiger. Then he could get the better of Kate.

'Nice being in the country.' Dad again. Wish he'd put a sock in it. Not even Steffi's interested. Dad's the one who was brought up out here. He's the one wanting to 'get in touch' with his roots. Can't think why. He hasn't got any. You only have to look at him to see that. Ordinary middle-aged Aussie guy. I'll even be going to the school he went to. Horrors. Imagine if there's some old teacher there that remembers him.

Hamilton's crunching; I can hear it above my music. No, it's Sher Khan.

'Do you think he ought to be eating those?' I pull out one ear bud.

'Of course not,' butts in Kate. 'If you don't want them, give them to me. Wasteful boy.'

Hamilton doesn't seem to have heard. He does that a lot. It doesn't fool me. One day it won't fool Kate either. I give her a look. Even I must seem like a second mother to him sometimes, but she's merciless. 'Pick this up, do that, wash your hands, you dirty boy. Stop picking your nose.' And she's only ten. Just then Sher Khan decides the Cheezels aren't coming quick enough. He makes a rush for the packet on Kate's lap.

'Hey.' The Cheezel bag goes flying, Hamilton's clutching for Sher Khan while Kate starts yelping. 'Gross. Now he's piddled on me. Hamilton, get this stinking animal off me.'

'Put him in his cage,' I hiss at Hamilton as the rabbit gets yanked off Kate's lap and housed by Hamilton's feet. Dad's obviously missed the point of the drama; even Steffi seems preoccupied.

'Don't worry, kids. It'll be lovely and green in May.' We're passing over some river. No water in it, of course, an old dray rotting in the sun. Deep inside of me I groan as I turn up my volume. I could have stayed with Auntie Joy.

Then I could have graduated at my own school, with my own friends. 'You'll make new friends,' Dad had said. 'And they'll be nicer in the country.' I knew he'd lost it by then.

Oh, why hadn't Great-aunt Dorie lived on some tropical island off Queensland? Why Kapunda?

I have to admit, Kapunda isn't as dry and dusty and derelict as I imagined. A huge statue of a miner stands tall as we drive in, guarding the place like some giant out of Kate's Celtic storybooks. Street signs advertise historical drives and the mine. Still a country town, though. Bet it's like a graveyard at the weekends. And I start thinking about Ben. Well, nothing much happening there, but it would have. Fat chance I've got now, seventy kilometres away from all the action.

Then we're turning up this old street. Same old main street in every country town. It's wide and the buildings look like something out of a Western. I can imagine a lady in a long grey dress, a white apron, mob cap on her head, carrying a basket, coming from the bakery. Stone houses, old mine chimney. That's more of the history bit, I expect.

'See, there it is.' Both Dad's hands are off the wheel, pointing. 'The one with the slag fence. I used to stay here when I was a kid. Oh, wow.'

Kate and Hamilton are straining for a look. I'm not excited like them; I just want to see what a slag fence is. But as we stop, all I notice is bits of black stuff cemented on top of the stone as though someone thought it would be a decoration. Dad thinks it's cool. 'Only slag fence around.

The mine's just over there, you see.' He's facing towards the tall brick chimney, sweeping his arm to include all the land 'north of Kapunda down to the sea.

The kids are out of the car, racing under a pepper tree up to the front verandah. Hamilton's in the rear as usual with Sher Khan. Kate has the key. It's so old and huge it pokes out from both sides of her fist as she runs. Dad's talking to Steffi in his calm 'it'll be okay' tone. He manages to turn it on sometimes. 'You'll like it here, Steffi, you'll see. You love old things and this is the perfect place to put all yours. It'll be better for us. It's restful.'

Yeah, right. They might like restful but what about me? Dad follows the kids up the garden and Steffi waits for me. I'm not leaving my iPod or iPad in the car, even if Dad says you don't have to lock anything out here. Out here. How can something like this happen to me? I must have groaned aloud because Steffi's got her arm around me. She's walking slowly, like me, and I feel as though we have something in common. We don't always, except for Dad and the two kids. We don't even look remotely alike, her with freckles and red hair and me with my nondescript dark brown, like Dad's must have been. Steffi and me, we're a bit careful with each other. She's not my real mum and every now and then we both seem to remember that at the same time. Even after twelve years, Dad's the one who tells me off, though Steffi handles all the girl stuff. Before we met Steffi it was just Dad and me. I don't remember my real mum, and Dad pointed out to me one day that Steffi is as real a mum as I'll ever get.

So I call her Mum to her face. She likes it, I know, just as we also know she's too young to have a daughter as old as me.

Dad's a kid again, calling out from the front verandah. 'Look at these verandah posts, Steffi. They're original, you know. This sort were only made here in the Hawke foundry. And the colour of the lime siltstone!' It looks like plain pink peeling stone to me, just an old crappy house with straggly white roses climbing up its posts, no great windows to look out from, no swimming pool, no —

Just then Kate comes screaming out the front door. 'Jenfa!' Both of them still call me that sometimes — a habit from baby days. 'Jenfa. Come quick. You'll never guess!'

'Oh yes,' I hear Dad say as I follow Kate inside the empty house. 'There's something I haven't mentioned …'

'There's downstairs!' Kate's pounding down ahead of me.

'Most old places have a cellar, Kate.'

'No. Look!'

And I look. At the bottom of the stairs, a slate floor stretches away from me. A rough wooden door with a wrought iron ring the size of a doughnut is right in front, then a door on each side. It's like an underground courtyard. The doors look like they were filched from a Gothic castle and I murmur in respect, 'There's a whole floor down here.'

Kate has my hand in a satisfied clutch. 'That's not it. Look at this.' She pulls me down the last of the stairs and into the room on the right. It's a sitting room of some sort. 'Look at the window, Jenfa. It's underground, but the light

8

still comes in, and there's a cupboard in the wall.' She opens it with a flourish to show me. There's a secret space behind. Big enough for her to hide in. How thick are these walls? I stand there blinking, but she's pulling me again. 'That's not all. Come on.' I get dragged into the room across the slate floor. 'There's a fireplace, see?'

The floor looks like powdery stone. The ceiling is the underbelly of the wooden floor above, crossed by wooden beams. There's a huge old dark bookcase on the wall. Another cupboard opens to reveal a recess. A ground-level bay window, bathed in a stream of light — a place I could put plants in. It's out of this world. And weird. I can imagine someone sitting there, reading or writing, a girl in a white cotton dress, long dark hair streaming down her back. A feeling begins to stir and uncurl inside me, one I don't recognise. All I know is I have to have this room.

'This could be mine, don't you think, Jenfa? And Hamilton could have the other one. Sher Khan would like being underground.' I'm surprised Kate thought of the rabbit, then I realise she's getting me on her side so I can come to her defence when she asks for the room. But this is one court case I'm not taking part in.

'Don't even think of it, Kate. Do you imagine Mum would let you two live underground? You'd get all white and pasty. It's most probably haunted anyway.'

Kate pales slightly. 'Oh?'

'Come on. Let's see where Hamilton is.' I find him at the other end of the house, above ground, putting Sher Khan's cage on a wide windowsill that proves just how thick the walls are. 'You like this room, Hamilton?'

He doesn't even turn. 'Sher Khan might keep wanting to get out of his cage if Kate and I slept underground.' The room is blue, has two windows — one looks across to church spires, the other out the front to the pepper tree.

'It's a lovely room, Hamilton. This house is bigger than it looks.' Kate hasn't followed me and I suddenly know where she is. I run down the hallway to the staircase. I hear her raised voice.

'But I'd make sure he didn't fall down the stairs.'

'Kate —' Steffi's voice.

I get down there as fast as I can. But I can't very well ask for the room, not in front of Kate. Not after she said she wanted it.

'Actually, I think this would make a very good room for Mum and me.' Dad's got that excited look again.

It's Steffi who notices the expression in my eyes. It surprises me that she can see how I feel. I'm usually more careful. Who wants everyone walking all over your life, which is what happens as soon as you let your guard down and try to tell people what you're feeling.

'Mark, don't you think Jenefer would be better down here? I'm not so fond of dim places and I like the room immediately above.'

There are more rooms? Then I let myself relax as Dad begins to scratch his stubble.

'Well, if you think so. It's just that I was never allowed

10

to sleep down here when I was a kid. It was all blocked off.'

'You can visit, Dad. In the room across there.' Now I grin. I'm experiencing something I haven't felt for at least a month. That uncurling again. I'm not sure what it is — interest? Hope that things will get better? Kate is pouting, and I decide there's room to be magnanimous. 'You can come for sleepovers if you like.' It doesn't work.

'You always get the best. Just because you were with Dad first!'

'Kate —' Steffi is following her up the stairs.

I try not to let it bother me; it was Steffi after all who said I could have the room.

The removal truck has been and I'm sitting in my heritage-listed underground bedroom, deciding how I'll arrange it. We've all ended up with a room of our own. Kate has the one next to Hamilton. Mum and Dad are above me. There's even a spare. The room across from me is just like an underground library — like those etchings in classical novels — it has our extra books and the computer in it. The computer is the only thing down here that reminds me I'm in the twenty-first century. Dad thought it best I have it near me since I'll use it the most for Year 12. Getting Kate off her games and Paint Master will be my biggest challenge. Maybe Steffi will let her have more time on her iPod.

I'm walking around the room, still stunned at the gift I've been given. That's what it feels like. School will no doubt be horrible. The kids, country hicks (the guys most probably line-dance and ride horses) and the town — well, what can you expect? But this room is going to be my haven, I can tell. My hand runs along the mantelpiece. Can you believe that? It even has a mantelpiece. Like it was a sitting room at one time. I've already put plants in the window space that has the light filtering down from outside. The secret cupboard (that everyone knows about) has my folders, DVDs and jewellery in it. I might be able to lock it. I'm just checking the possibilities of that when my hand catches on a sharp end of the bookcase. Ouch! I pull my hand away suddenly but not before I feel the thing shudder.

I stop a moment, then stretch out and pull. The whole bookcase is on hinges! It swings right out from the wall. And inside is another stone space deep enough to hide in. At least to stash stuff in. Incredible. And no one knows about it. No one at all. I close it quickly in case someone comes. Wouldn't do to have Kate know. All of the primary school would follow her home to have a squiz. I sit down on the bed and think. What sort of house is this? Secret compartments. A whole floor underground. Well, two big rooms and a smaller one, which Dad will fill with wine and photographic equipment. He's never taken to digital cameras and loves developing photos like in the dark ages. Dad said this used to be a manse. They didn't need priest holes in Australia, surely? Not like in English history when it was dangerous to be Catholic, like Steffi with her crucifix above the bed. Though Steffi would have been safe. She never goes to mass; just chooses all the wrong moments to remember those rules she learnt. Dad's family has almost always lived here, he said. That's why he was so set on us coming. And I don't remember any talk about them being Catholic.

I can't work it out so I put everything away instead. Already I'm starting to think of stories and scenarios that could have happened here. It's just that sort of place.

It's at night when I wonder if I've chosen so well. Once the light goes out I settle down. It's my bed, my pillow. Everything should be fine. The house becomes quiet, like an aviary after dark. Steffi's stopped creaking around upstairs. The kids were in bed ages ago. Dad's like the dead when he sleeps, so when I first hear this tiny noise I know it's nothing human. Knock. Tap. Scratch. A hollow sound — not the noisy scuffling that mice make, but scraping, scratching. A sound miniature people would make in the skirting boards if they were trying to escape. Fairies? God help me. Scratch. Tap. It stops at times. Once it stopped for a whole half-hour, I'm sure of it.

That's when I think it's finished and I drop off to sleep. But my dreams are troubled with images of all the horror stories I've ever read. Little people, green men with wings, laughing and drawing me to a cliff edge where I know I'll have to jump to the rocks below to escape them. When I look down, the water's so wild. The waves, white with anger, are smashing up on the rocks and cliff, snatching for me with long fingers of foam; the grass is a vibrant green even in the black of night.

My sheets are wet with sweat when I wake. It's early and I listen. No tapping, but the house is alive already. Dad's made coffee; the smell even wafts its way down here. Kate's voice is coming closer, telling Hamilton off about something.

'Jenfa. Are you awake? Can I come down?' She's down anyway. I struggle up as she jumps on the bed.

'Careful.'

'What's wrong with you? We've been up forever.'

'Nothing's wrong. Kate?'

'Hmm?' Her bright little eyes are surveying my room. No doubt deciding where her stuff would go if she were here. I don't want her catching on to the movable bookcase. 'Can you get me your storybook. The one Auntie Joy gave you about Celtic fairies and myths?'

She turns this interested look on me.

'I want to write something and I want to get the facts right. OK?'

'Sure.' While she's gone I get dressed and head up into the kitchen. Steffi's there at the stove.

'Mum? Do you reckon there's another dimension?' She's staring at me, egg slice in midair. 'You know. Ghosts.'

She's flipping the eggs now, lips pursed. 'Not me, Jenefer.' Then she grins. 'But your Aunt Dulcie swore there was someone here.'

'Dulcie?'

'Your dad's aunt who died years ago. The one who used to live here with Dorie.'

'And you came here? Knowing that?'

Steffi chuckles. It's such a nice normal sound. 'She was old, Jenefer. And starting to lose her faculties. Who'd take notice?'

I would, I think. After last night. 'Are you all right, Jenefer? Sleep well?'

'Sure.' There must be some explanation. With any luck, I imagined it.

This is the third day I've woken up in what should be a state of wellbeing. Even plain boredom would be preferable. I don't even have the energy to miss my friends properly. I'm definitely starting to look haggard. It must be bad; Dad's noticed. He reckons I'll settle soon. Normally I'd have a go at him about that. 'Settle soon' as if I was a little kid. It'd take all year for sure and then it'd be time for me to go back to uni in Adelaide. But right now I'm not even thinking about what I left behind. If only that's all it was. That infernal scratching when the house goes quiet. So faint — just loud enough so you know something is there. Kate's book doesn't help much; full of mermaids and giants. So I go down to the library. I thought it would be scary enough walking to the shops where everyone's going to know I'm from the 'new family' just moved in. But ghostly scraping in the middle of the night beats even that.

I find this old book by a Robert Hunt written centuries ago about fairies and demons. It's really hard to read, with words not used anymore. I can't believe there are so many kinds of fairies and piskies, and this is just a book on Cornwall. I see this bit about fairies and changelings — how human babies can be changed for a fairy one if they're sickly or not looked after. So creepy.

Then suddenly I see it. *The fairy miners — the knockers.* Knockers! This is it. I just know it. *These are the sprites of the mines. They are not allowed to rest because of their wicked practices as tinners. Souls who are too good for hell, too bad for heaven. Small withered creatures, large ugly heads with old men's faces. Spiteful if crossed.* I shiver. Our house is almost next to the old mine. Could some have tunnelled across? Jenefer, get a grip! What am I thinking of? No one believes this stuff anymore. It's just stories for kids. Superstitions that ignorant people used in the old days to make sense of their world. Right, Jenefer. But what about the tapping you can hear at night?

I can't bear to read any more. Nor do I take the book out. For some reason, I don't want it in my room, as though its presence will make the knockers real. And in the daylight I don't believe they are. Honest. The librarian smiles at me, but I make a quick getaway. Bet she's wondering why I haven't joined but I don't feel like talking. I can't wait to escape to the house. If only I could go back home and to my school at Cedar Rise with all my old friends. No knockers there.

It's when I'm coming out of the heavy old wooden doors that I first notice the guy. He's across the road, coming out of the Post Office. There's this huge mural all over the outside wall with horses, colours, a beautiful old house. It's like he's painted there too. He sees me looking and waves. I freeze. No one waves at you where I used to live. In Italy they clap at you, apparently — saw it on a movie — and I've had a wolf whistle from a car full of hoons once. But no one's waved. He's got to be weird, and I walk off towards the house, but on the way I remember how he looked. Dark, and not just his hair. His smile was friendly and white, and he wore torn jeans. Cool. But he waved. He may as well have bowed.

By the end of the week, I can't stand it anymore. I tell Steffi there are knockers in my bedroom. 'Do you hear tapping in the night, Mum?'

She gives me this sharp look. 'No, Jenefer.' She's not asking if I do, but I can tell it's an effort for her not to. So I say it.

'I can hear this dull scratchy sort of knocking behind the wall. Hollow tapping.' I almost say like miniature picks, but stop in time. 'It's so spooky. Not loud. I can only hear it when everything goes quiet. I've tried going to sleep earlier but it doesn't work — I'm waiting for it to start.' Steffi still hasn't said anything. 'You don't suppose Aunt Dulcie was right, do you?'

Steffi smiles then. 'No, Jenefer. I'll ask your father.'

'He'll think I'm stupid,' I wail.

'I won't tell him what you think it is. Only what you heard.'

'There's a difference?'

'Maybe.'

Dad knows straight away. He's horrified. 'Hell, Jenefer. You heard scratching?'

I nod, determined not to be frightened by his tone. I hate it when he gets too loud. He doesn't sound scared, but he isn't pleased either. His voice is rising like it always does when he's annoyed or frustrated. I don't want it to affect me; at least I hope it's not directed at me. Not like when he got stuck into me at the end of last year for sneaking into a night club with Amy after the exams. I got so frightened and angry I shouted back at him. And burst into tears. It was so humiliating. The scariest thing this time is that he's not questioning what I heard. He believes me!

'This is going to cost so much money.'

'What will, Mark?' Steffi's sewing up green velvet curtain hems with pins in her mouth. And talking in nice soft tones, like he's got all the reason in the world to be aggro. Good one, Steffi.

'Getting rid of them.' Dad sounds slightly mollified;

he's being understood at last. I don't have Steffi's talent for Dad-soothing. Maybe I get a stubborn look on my face or something; I can never quieten him down.

And now I'm heaps spooked. How do you get rid of knockers in the twenty-first century? I wonder if Robert Hunt really believed all the stories he wrote about and whether there will have to be exorcisms or something to clear knockers out of someone's basement.

'So how will we do it, Dad?' I'm watching Steffi calmly put all the pins back in the black film container. She's tired of hemming.

'Get the pest control man, I suppose.' He sighs like it's going to physically hurt.

'The pest control man?' And Steffi laughs.

'It's no laughing matter, Steffi. Could cost a couple of thousand in an old place like this.'

I still haven't caught on, though the scary part has passed. Steffi's looking at me with her eyes brimming, the curtain totally forgotten. 'So what will the pest control man do?' I ask as Steffi starts to splutter again.

'Get rid of the white ants.' Then Dad's eyes narrow as he looks at me. 'That was the knocking, Jenefer. When they gnaw the wood you can hear it.' He's being sarcastic; Kate would have just said 'duh'. I can tell it's on the tip of his tongue to ask what on earth I thought the scratching was, but how was I supposed to know? Our house in Adelaide was relatively new. Nothing like white ants ever happened.

Steffi steers him to the phone. 'Better do it then, eh, Mark?'

Dad sighs. 'Only trouble with old houses — all the maintenance.'

'But you wanted it,' she reminded him.

'Yeah, yeah. You can't let a piece of history like this fall to wrack and ruin. This was built in 1858, you know.'

With a heap of relief, I escape to my newly exorcised room.

Apparently, it's best to be out when there's a white ant man fumigating your house. My job is to take Kate and Hamilton to the duck pond. It's not so far. Kate packed a picnic but she wouldn't let Hamilton help. Just hope she put enough food in for all three of us. We're crossing the main street, near the antique shop, when this run-down rusty ute suddenly parks right in our path. My eyes are reading 'Camel Farm, Kapunda' on the door as the Waving Guy gets out and says 'Hi'. I'm still walking round the front of the ute, onto the footpath, but Kate stops and says 'Hi' back. I could kill her. It's not that he looks dangerous or anything — up close he looks fine, more than fine — but it's embarrassing. He talks to Kate instead.

'You're new to town, then?' Wish it wasn't so obvious, and it rankles that he says it conversationally, like he already knows.

'Yes.' Kate answers in her best I'm-ten-going-on-sixteen voice.

'Looking forward to school on Monday?'

Kate nods, though I can tell she doesn't want to be reminded of only being in Year 5 at the moment.

'So am I,' the Waving Guy adds.

I pull my head up at this. He seems older. He's looking at me now, waiting for me to say something. Well, he can wait. Damn Kate though.

'Are you in Year 12? Jenefer's in Year 12.' Thanks a million, Kate. Now he knows everything. I grab her arm and Hamilton's and walk them round the corner to where Dad said this pond was.

'Ow, Jenfa. You're hurting. And you're rude. Why didn't you say something? He was nice.'

'You can't tell when you just meet someone if they're nice. You should be more careful.'

'But Dad said everyone was nice in Kapunda. It's the country.' This from Hamilton who usually is careful. I sigh in frustration. No wonder kids get abducted.

'Everybody waves. See?' And just as Hamilton says this, the guy drives past, waving again and grinning.

'What do you mean, "everybody waves"?' I ask, even though I've caught on. I've seen outback shows on TV; I just didn't realise it would happen here.

Hamilton's determined to be patient with me, I can tell. 'Dad said people wave in the country to be friendly.' And suddenly I feel as if I've crossed a border to an unknown land.

On the other side of this border I have no idea what to do or when to do it, whether to shake hands, spit at people or wave. In Adelaide you can't wave to a guy. He'd think you were weird or on the make. Now this guy must think I'm a snob.

At least the pond is like any other pond, with wild ducks, reeds and decking that stretches out into the water. Hamilton and Kate spend most of the time feeding crumbs to the baby ones. 'I don't think they should have too much of that,' I say after I remember all the signs in the Botanical Gardens about not feeding bread to black swans.

'Don't give them so much!' I hear Kate's voice floating back, bossy as though she thought of it herself. I lean back and watch through half-closed eyes. One of these days I'll rip into Kate for the way she treats Hamilton, but I'm always hoping he'll do it himself. Surely it can't be good for him to have someone like me stick up for him all the time? Then I hear giggling.

Three girls my age are strolling by. They look relaxed, sharing quiet, intimate stuff. I hear a few snatches — they're still at school, that much I can tell. They look like they'd never need a new friend. This is going to be so hard. How do you make friends at a school where they've all grown up together? Dad reckons they'll be friendly. Like the waving thing, I guess. But he doesn't know teenage girls. Being brought up on a farm or in a little town can't change human nature that much, can it?

When we get back to the house, everything's upside down, in more ways than one.

'Guess what?' Steffi looks even more excited than Dad was when we came. Usually he's the only crazy one with his roller-coaster moods, and Steffi helps to smooth his fur down. 'We have a secret room!'

Kate shrieks. 'Where? Can I see?' Hamilton just blinks and waits for more information. Honestly, he's starting to look like Sher Khan.

'Next to Jenefer's room.'

Kate throws me a dart of pure jealousy. I'm just glad we didn't know about it before I found out what the knocking was. 'Under the stairs.' So we all troop down to have a look. Dad's already there, standing by this round hole less than a metre across. He's got his cordless drill, screwing a board across the top with a square of curtain material stapled to it.

'The pest control man found it. He noticed this part of the wall looked tampered with so he dug in with a hammer and chisel, and it went straight through.'

'Must have been a door here sometime,' Steffi adds, 'and over the years it got plastered up.'

'Wow.' You can always tell how impressed Kate is by the decrease in the number of words she can manage.

'But you can't go in, Kate.'

I see the rebel look that flashes over her features before she presents them to Dad. 'It's so dark you can't see anything. It'll be full of spiders.'

'Or snakes,' I add for Kate's benefit. Dad looks at me with his eyelids half down. He's warning me to be careful, too. But this is one thing I would have to do. Alone. And before Kate does. A secret room and not go in? Impossible. This house is getting more interesting by the day. If I'm not careful, I'll even be getting into the family stuff, like Great-aunt Dorie.

I've waited until the kids are in bed. Kate's been watching me like a hungry eagle ever since tea. I was so busy trying not to look excited that I couldn't even eat my chops, while Dad was going on about how lucky it was 'only the skirting boards'. After tea he went outside to put some order in his new shed before he got too busy at the uni admin office to even think about it. I stayed up in the lounge with Steffi and she wanted me to play the piano. Hamilton loves it when I do. Whenever I finish a piece I can hear his thin, sleepy voice all the way down the hall like a prisoner in a dungeon: 'Play some more.' The 'more' gets all drawn out like he's on the rack. It's touching really, when he's the one that has the talent and he doesn't realise. He can pick out a song the next day that he's heard me play the night before. Without even reading the music.

Finally, they're all quiet. I've got the rechargeable torch. Down at the bottom of the stairs, I stare at the piece of material Dad's hung there. Dare I? There's no such things as knockers, or little people, or ghosts. Go on, Jenefer Tremayne. What are you waiting for? I've tied my hair back, just in case there's sticky stuff hanging in there. So disgusting. Dad says it possibly hasn't seen the light of day since the 1860s. I try not to think about spiders and all sorts of other life forms that like the dark. I lift the material up first and shine the torch in. Dad may be right and there's nothing there. I see the stone walls; old wooden beams. Nothing much, really. Looks like I don't need to venture in after all. Then the light catches on something. I bring the arc of light back. There's a shadow. I still don't move. It's an odd shape, sort of lumpy. Obviously nothing to do with the stone wall.

Now I have to go and find out what it is. I'm always like this — can be scared witless but I have to find out. If there was a snake lying beside the last clue to a puzzle, I reckon I'd go for it. I crawl in through the hole. Dribbles of stone and rock run down the wall. I stop but no one comes. No creaks from the floorboards in Steffi and Dad's room above. When I'm through the hole I stand upright, and shine the torch around some more. The air is musty; sure hope I don't get sick like those people who first opened that ancient tomb in the pyramids. At least this air is only 150 years old. It all seems fairly clear in here except for the Shadow. I creep over, slowly. Don't want to upset any little animals that call this home. I hear one tiny scuttle and a swish but that's all and I start breathing more easily. The Shadow isn't moving; it's just some inanimate object. Covered with a blanket the same colour as the wall. That might be why Dad never noticed it. I drag off the blanket, paper thin, and then I see the box. It's so eerie in the torch light it makes me take a deep breath. This is no ordinary box. I run my hand over the top, the roof; it's a house. There's even a door, and windows. Something round on the side. It looks about half a metre wide. I glance back at the hole. Will I get it through? I suddenly know I have to; I can't leave this box here.

I try lifting it but it's so heavy. Made from solid old wood, like the old pine Steffi makes things out of. She would love it; she's always sniffing in antique shops, finding things she can do up. The lounge is testimony to her dedication to furniture restoration. The coffee table she even made from old floor boards. I try half-dragging, half-lifting. The dust is floating up from the floor — little puffs of it — it's a hundred and fifty years thick. I know I'll sneeze soon and a sneeze will not be a good idea rising up from the bowels of the house into Steffi and Dad's room. Finally I use the blanket. It's a dust trap too, but I manage to get it under the box by lifting one corner at a time, and gently drag the blanket across the floor. The stone isn't too even and the box keeps catching. I hear a rip, like old autumn leaves that snap in your hand. I just hope the box makes it to the opening in one piece. It does. Then I half-stumble through and drag the blanket behind me. That only works until the top of the box hits the stone above the opening, with a pile of crumbly stone dribbling onto the floor. I have a go at scraping away some more of the stone to make the hole bigger before I can part-lift and part-drag the box through. I'm trying to do all this quietly, hoping Dad won't notice the hole's not quite the same.

It's the middle of the night before I get the box safely into my room. It's been dusted and I decide to put it in my secret cupboard behind the bookcase — the only secret place left that no one knows about. Before I do, I have a good look at it in the light of the lamp. It's a house for sure, like an old-fashioned doll's house. Set on a wall with a gabled roof and a waterwheel on the side. The wheel does a half-turn before it catches on something. Little windows are set into the wood. The door moves slightly but it won't open. I sit for what seems like hours, letting the magic of it seep into me. My finger moves slowly round each feature; it's beautifully crafted. Who would make something so lovely then hide it in a secret underground room? The roof doesn't lift off, like I thought it might, and I don't want to force it. I wonder if it's sacrilege to open it at all. Finally, I slip into my bed.

It's Monday morning. The Monday morning. When I will find out how wrong Dad's been. The school's moved on a bit since the nineteen-seventies, I bet. I still haven't told Steffi and Dad about the box. I'll have to sooner or later, I guess, especially since I haven't worked out how to open it yet. Dad will try and he might wreck it with that 'I can do anything'

male thing he gets at times. Besides, it's still too precious and mysterious. I need to savour that a little longer.

I've seen the school from the road and once, a few months ago, I even came for an interview. But nothing's prepared me for seeing it close-up on a Monday morning. With kids everywhere. All in blue. That's another thing. Cedar Rise school had such a great uniform — like none at all. Now I have nowhere to go. I know nothing, except the office. At least I know where that is: across this stretch of lawn with pepper trees loudly whispering like water withdrawing on a very shelly beach. Piles of kids are standing or sitting around, catching up, smiling, happy — belonging, whether they like it or not. This is the pits; even the scared little first years will be better off than me. They'll at least have their friends from primary school with them.

I make my way up these marble steps inlaid with old Victorian tiles, trying to look like I've done this every single day for the last four years. Look interested in the tiles, Jenefer, maroon and green diamonds. This isn't like a school at all but a huge old house; donated by a cattle king, Dad said.

'Jenefer.' A few heads turn, mine included. Someone else named Jenefer? Uh-oh. Just as I feared: who alone in Kapunda knows my name? The Waving Guy. I take a few deep breaths as he walks over. This has got to be better than not knowing anyone at all, except they'll all think I only like guys. It's the girls you have to make it with to have a decent life at school. I can hear a wind and it has nothing to do with the pepper trees. Some older girls lean together. I don't know the protocol here. Do I go to class with him? Or ask the way? Or just accept his kindness, which, by the look on his face, is what I'm going to get.

'Wanna know where to go?'

'I don't know which class I'm in. I was heading for the office.' If he realises this is the first time I've spoken to him, he doesn't let on.

'Year 12?' I nod.

'Three home groups. But we all meet in the Year 12 room first. C'mon.' For one panic-stricken moment I thought he was going to pick up my bag. In my last school if a guy carried your bag it only meant one thing. And I don't even know him.

'Um, I still don't know your name.'

He throws me this side look, pauses; guess he remembers it's not his fault I don't know his name. I feel my face go hot as I think he's not going to answer, but then he looks back to the front and keeps walking. 'It's Caleb.'

'You're in Year 12 too?' Dumb, Jenefer. Of course I know he's in Year 12.

And he grins back at me as I catch up. 'Year 13 actually. They suggested I do Year 12 over two years — three subjects each year.' He says 'suggested' like he was forced into it. I can imagine the sessions that teachers call career-counselling.

'I'm thinking of doing that too.' I have a hazy recollection of bikes tied up as we walk round the old mansion. Pale stone and the old iron lacework that Dad raves on about, painted the tuscany colour he likes. Lots of kids in this part too; guys in grey trousers or shorts are kicking a footy around.

'Really? It suits me, I guess. This way I can work part-time.'

'The camel farm?' I ask, half-trying to show I'm not as snobby as I acted last week and half-wondering what sort of guy likes camels. I've never even seen one close up. And I thought horses were hicksville.

'Yeah.' But he doesn't elaborate. 'What subjects you doing?'

'English, History, IT —'

'They your favourites?'

I nod. I don't mention I wanted to do classics.

'I left my favourites till this year,' he carries on. I don't say anything. 'To keep me comin' back.' He's grinning again and I ask the obvious. 'So what are they?' Looking at him I can't tell — not IT, I bet.

'Art, Ag Science, PE.'

This floors me. Art? I look up at him; I can't imagine that at all. Ag Science and camels, yes; he looks wild enough to jump on one, his hair just that bit too long and unruly for a private city school. Suddenly I can imagine it flying in the wind as he gallops away somewhere into the sand dunes. I stop myself in time. Gallops? Is that what camels do?

'Did you take English last year?' I'm actually feeling disappointed he won't be in any of my classes. For a little while I thought I had a blow-up lifebuoy in a choppy bay. Now it has a puncture and it's going down fast.

'Nope. Why learn the language of the conquerors, eh?' He's chuckling, but there's an undercurrent to it I can't define. So he is Aboriginal, or Indigenous as we keep getting told. With that smile and skin — though it's hard to tell with some people. His skin is even lighter than Rasheed's in my class last year.

'Besides —' Caleb says, 'they should teach First Australian languages.'

I'm not sure about all this; it's the way he says 'First Australian'. There's no sting — at least I don't feel one directed at me — but why did he mention it? I've never had an Indigenous friend. Sokha was one of my best friends at Cedar Rise — Khmer, from Cambodia — and I miss her, especially right now. I knew Rasheed well, even went to his house, under the guise of being his sister's friend. Totally platonic, but he said his parents wouldn't understand platonic. Ate shish kebabs and hot naan from the oven. But so many of the kids at my last school never knew anything about Indigenous people. Except for the homeless ones in Victoria Square. Sokha, Amy and I would get off the bus to go to the market and walk the long way round in case any of the Indigenous people there touched us for money. It was a horrible feeling, wanting to help but not knowing if giving money would. Maybe they wouldn't have asked anyway; it was just our fear. Fear of the unknown.

Conquerors, he said. I've never thought about it like

that before. The British just settled a country, didn't they? They didn't swoop over in ships after years of planning like Alexander the Great, mowing down everybody in their path, leaving their green eyes and fair skin behind, did they? Then I look at Caleb again. His eyes aren't as dark as they might have been. This could get complicated. Languages, he said.

'So you know one? A First Australian language?'

He's serious now. 'Only a bit. It's mostly lost.' And suddenly we're there in this transportable room. I see the lounge chairs, a wide grey dividing screen. Guys are slapping Caleb on the back. 'Caleb, you black piker, you came back after all. Tim lost his bet.' Caleb's grinning. All the guy stuff's making me uncomfortable; it's just normal camaraderie, I guess, but I'm not used to it.

'This is Jenefer. They've just moved into the old manse.' That makes me gasp; how does he know where I live? But before I can ask, a girl moves over. With relief I recognise her — one of the girls walking past the duck pond on Saturday. Maybe she did notice me sitting there.

'Hi, I'm Erin,' and she guides me to the other end of the room, behind the screen. It's set up as a class and I wonder how teachers survive the noise level if kids have frees in the lounge part.

'Jenefer,' I answer, still not sure what else to say. Then she smiles. 'You looked like you needed rescuing. Caleb can be a bit full-on.'

'He was kind,' is all I can come up with. He doesn't

seem as weird as I thought during the week.

'Yes, well,' and her eyebrows rise, as if he's not her type. She seems nice enough though, and she takes English.

'I wanted to do Classics.' I hope I don't look as teary as I feel.

She sighs in sympathy. 'So did I. But it's History here. Classics isn't offered this year. Not enough lines in the timetable.'

'Can't we do it anyway?' I'm starting to get desperate. This wouldn't have happened in the city. I've never even thought before how timetables and subjects got sorted out. They were always just there, so many, ready for the choosing.

'Don't worry. We have more subjects offered here than any other country school.' And I'm supposed to feel consoled? Just wait until I tell Dad how he's ruined my education.

The day isn't too bad, I guess; Erin sticks with me at lunch and the girls do seem nicer than I'd thought. One called Ashleigh comes from a farm, but they've only been in the district a few years, Erin says, as though the other girl can't help it. Why should she tell me that when I've been here less than two weeks? Another girl called Alicia lives 'on the land' too, but I don't get to talk to her. Yet another, Lauren, tells me all about netball and how the way to get to know people in Kapunda is to play it. Tough luck — I don't play, but I don't say so. I find myself wanting them to like me, yet I can't tell if they do. There's a polite wall around most of them that I can see even Ashleigh hasn't scaled; they smile but it's like they're ready with the artillery if I should say anything against the area. As if I'd be that stupid. But it's hard thinking of things to say that I imagine won't offend, and my head's like Neptune's whirlpool by home time when Caleb turns up in the Year 12 lounge again. His sneakers look like he's been watering the garden.

'I'll walk down the street with you, if you want.' He says it lightly so I can take it or leave it and this is my cue to say I don't need him to walk back with me; that I know where to go, but I don't. There's something about him I like; can't put my finger on it, but I feel like finding out what it is. Besides, no one's warned me off him. Erin wasn't all that encouraging, but wouldn't she have said if he was sus? We would have at Cedar Rise, if a new girl was being annoyed by the class drop-kick. Though for all I know this is the country girl's idea of revenge: let the city girl find out the hard way what's acceptable and what isn't.

On the way I decide to ask Caleb about his art. This is the best way I can think of to get to know him, if I can.

'Mum's an artist. She taught me all she knows about colour, the land, how it's important.' He turns to me then. 'She's from the Stolen Generation.'

It's a piece of information that I realise he doesn't have to part with and thankfully I know what he's talking about. I'd read *The Burnt Stick* when I was a kid. Got told all that stuff at school about Sorry Day. But I still don't know what is a suitable comment. Should I say, *Really?* Like how interesting, or should I sound horror-struck and say how terrible it was for the Brits to do what they did. But I'm a Brit, aren't I? Australian, yet Dad's people came over on a boat at some stage. I should ask Dad. Caleb seems to know so much about who he is, and I have no idea. I just hang in the air of time on a cobweb that could break so easily.

'Was your father an artist too?'

Caleb hesitates slightly. 'Nah, he was a farmer, but he didn't understand about the land, Mum said. He wasn't a Nunga.' Then he looks at me. 'Same as you.'

'Me?'

'Yeah.' He's not looking at me now; it's like he's talking about the price of oranges and lemons. 'You're a Goonya.'

I've never thought about it. Some instinct tells me not to say that aloud and I'm glad. He adds, 'Did you meet Alicia Tilbrook today?'

The tossing, blonde-haired vision that was Alicia in History class comes to mind, and I nod slightly. You couldn't say I met her exactly. 'You take Alicia. She doesn't know she's an immigrant Australian. Lives on a thousand acres but wouldn't understand she walks on someone's spirit home.'

'What does she think she is?' I ask, nervous. It's a bit too close to the bone. All of a sudden, I'm not sure what he's talking about. Wonder if he guesses. Why is he telling me? Is all this just for my benefit or to test me out?

'She's just never thought about it. She knows she's normal, and everyone else is a shade different in comparison. Like I'm a Nunga.'

What do I say? I look up at him. You couldn't call him black, really; his skin's like an Italian's who's been on the beach all summer.

He spreads his hands, explaining. 'It's what I am. It's cool.'

Mentally, I gulp. How long before he catches on I'm no different to Alicia Tilbrook?

'But you, Jenefer.' He stops then, and we're standing on the footpath; a lone car goes past, and all I can do is stare at him, wait for his next word. 'You're different.' Different from what? Alicia? And why is he saying it anyway? He can't possibly know.

'How do you know that?' Now I'm sure he's stringing me along. It might be his way of finding out what I think about him; his way to pick up the new chick in town. Guess he'd have to have some sort of strategy since Alicia must think he's a try-hard. Why else would he pick on her? And once a girl like that doesn't like a guy, how can anyone else?

'I can tell.'

'How?' I'm not letting him get away with this one.

We start walking again. 'Last week? When you wouldn't talk to me?'

I'm sure my face is flushing. 'So?'

'I knew it wasn't 'cos I was a Nunga. You had a different look in your face. It was just because I was a guy and you were annoyed about something, I reckon. I could handle that.'

I grin. 'Actually, it was the waving.'

'What?' He stops to stare at me.

'In Adelaide nice guys don't wave at girls they don't

36

know … as far as I know,' I suddenly add, in the face of his unexpected embarrassment.

'And nor do nice girls return the favour, right? Hell, I'm sorry. I didn't realise.'

'It's OK.' We're both laughing now, walking, and this is when I say it.

'Would you like to come home for a while? There's something I want to show you.'

I can't pinpoint the moment when I knew I wanted to share the box with Caleb; maybe it was all he said that gave me this feeling that the preciousness of it will be safe with him.

'A secret room?' he asks and I show him. Not that we can see anything — I forgot the torch. Caleb has just the right amount of wonder in his tone. He whistles. 'Cool.'

I can't imagine too many guys from Cedar Rise looking even remotely interested, let alone giving the attention Caleb's focusing on the hidden room. And then the box. We drag it out of my secret spot, not secret anymore, but I think it's worth it. He runs his hands over the roof. Just like I did. Yet why should he? At least I know the box is possibly something to do with my family. It's like he can read my mind.

'Your ancestor left this here?'

'I don't know. I'm not sure how to open it without

wrecking it.' I just hope it's not something like a pinyata or ceramic money box: to get the money out, you have to trash it, never any use again. Caleb's found the bits that move. He moves the wheel too. I watch him without breathing but I needn't have worried — he doesn't force it when it catches.

'There's a guy I've met at the camel races.' Camel races? I'm trying to look interested, but I'm restless, waiting to find out the connection between boxes and camels. Caleb glances up at me; he's still touching the box like it's a nervous horse and he's trying to discover what's hurting inside. 'Comes every year. He's an Indian hawker. Once he had a box with a trick opening.' Of course.

'He showed me one day. He kept his smokes in it. Probably a bit more besides.' Caleb grins again, then he concentrates. 'He used to slide one bit, then another came down and then it clicked open.'

I'm holding my breath again and it's not only because of the box. My heart is spinning just watching Caleb's hands. His fingers are long, brown, light underneath, pressing here, tugging a little there. Gentle. Paintbrushes, camels, what else has he touched to give that impression he's caressing, drawing secrets out of a box?

All of a sudden the wall under the house slides across, and under the waterwheel I can see something. 'There's a drawer. With a white knob.'

'Give it a pull.' Caleb leans back a bit as I tug. It's cool, smooth, ceramic. It doesn't move. Caleb's trying the roof, the wall again. That's when I think of the waterwheel.

'The wheel, Caleb. Try the wheel.' We reach out together, my hand brushes his, and he pulls back, reluctantly. He remembers it's my box. I turn the wheel just as we had before. Before it caught. Now it turns all the way and I watch astounded as the drawer slides out, jerking, with a weird clicking sound. Just like clockwork. Caleb leans over to see what's inside.

'A key.' My voice is little more than a whisper. It's made of iron, almost as big as the front door key. I pick it up. Heavy, too. It reaches all the way from my thumb to my little finger. 'What's it for?'

'Another secret room?'

I turn excited eyes onto Caleb. 'You think so?' But he shakes his head.

'We haven't finished with the box yet, Jenefer.'

'Okay, push the drawer in.'

Caleb turns the wheel this time and the drawer disappears with more clicks, like a sci-fi machine with a mind of its own. He tries sliding the wall back into place, but nothing spectacular happens. It's when he's pushing the wall the other way that I notice the gap in the wood. 'The wall's in two parts. Look. Just move one.' We keep the part still that's hiding the drawer and move the one on the left. As soon as it's slid from under the door, the door drops down with a clatter.

'There's your secret room, Jenefer.' I bend down and underneath the eaves is a keyhole. Just the right size. I don't say anything; just put the key in, turn it to the right, once, then again, and it clicks. I glance at Caleb. He's looking uncomfortable. Can't think why. I lift up the roof, and lean it back. The hinges are almost black, curly and beautiful. Then I look inside. I'd die if there was nothing at all. But there is. A packet of some sort, a small leather case, papers. I hesitate, not daring to touch them. Then Caleb stands up, backs away a step.

'This is something you need to do by yourself. If it's to do with your family, then it's special, stuff you need to find out. My mother would call it your dreaming.'

He says all this so sincerely that my eyes feel hot and prickly. He's right, I do want to look at it by myself; I'm just so touched that he understands. I shut my door and walk him up the stairs. I want to thank him for his help but it's been more than that. We've shared something I can't put a name to. I don't know what to do; what to say that won't sound ordinary. In the end, on the verandah, Caleb just flashes me his wide smile. 'See you tomorrow,' I think he says, but it's the smile I remember, like he knows everything that's in my head and he's pleased about it.

The house is quiet. No more knocking. No more tapping. The kids are in bed; this is the best time — not just for reading or writing poetry and all the other things I do when I'm supposed to be writing essays — but for looking in an ancient box that has reached out to me over two centuries.

That sounds so Emily Brontë, I know, but there's no other way to describe how I feel about this. Never before did I think I'd be affected by something from the past. I mean I love history, but not our own past. Great-aunt Dorie and even Dad were always going on about family history and I never listened; it sounded so boring. No secret affairs or duels at dawn.

Now I wish I'd paid attention. None of these names mean what they should. I have a photo-like card in my hand: *Miss Zenna Dare*. Who was Zenna Dare? I've never heard of her. She looks important, done up to the gills with feathers on her furry hat. Lace all over her dress. She's smiling, which looks odd for those times. No one used to smile in those old photos. Why is she? She doesn't seem much older than me.

Then there's this one: *Gweniver Rundle*. Unsmiling, proper. She has to be a relative. There was a Gweniver Tremayne; I can remember Dad mentioning her, at least. Think I was named after her. Our names mean the same. His great-gran, maybe? She looks familiar — not the family likeness thing — I've seen someone like her recently. There are more photos. They look like miniature paintings. Some from someone initialled 'R' to this Zenna Dare. I turn over a picture, black and white, colour lightly painted on, of a boat in the middle of a lake.

My dear Zenna, Why did you not come? I waited till 7.50 p.m. Will be at the Tea Gardens Sunday at 7 p.m. prompt. Please do not leave it like this. R

The writing is hard to read, though I think I've got it right. This must have been sent in an envelope. Then I see one, an envelope addressed to Gweniver Rundle, Fore Street, Camborne, Cornwall. Is this the one? I can't find any addressed to Zenna Dare.

I put all the pictures in the envelope and open the package next. It's a white dress, lace round the collar, and layers of it all the way down to the V waist. What sort of person wore clothes like this? I'm afraid to unfold it totally for fear it disintegrates into a puff of nothing, so I smell it instead. It's a mixture of moth balls and some perfume I can't exactly define, a fragrance of lavender. Old English gardens. My imagination is on a rampage: I can almost see Gweniver in this dress, what she'd look like, her hair half up on her head and half in a long dark ringlet on each side held with bows. Where would she be? In a garden? By the sea? What was Camborne like? And Cornwall? A land of moors and wild coasts?

There's more than a dress: a playbill announcing a ball and concert with all the players listed, the paper almost brown. A Miss Dare is one of them. Then there's the writing case filled with letters and papers. The leather is slightly ripped at the back and one of the tiny brass screws is missing from the hinge. All the papers out of order too; some with dates, some not. So weird, the paper looks like it's been screwed up and smoothed out again; some ripped-up pieces.

Too hard to know what to examine first, and it's late. So I lay the things out reverently in the box: the dress first, the leather case next; the photos on top. I sit here staring a while longer. I know there's something happening. I wish I had a red rosebud to lay on the photos. But since I don't, I close the lid, lock it, push the door up and slide the wall over. It's an effort by myself; so easy when Caleb was here. I hide the key back in the drawer under the water wheel, close the secret bookcase and slip into bed.

It's not until I'm too far asleep to get out again that I realise what I noticed about the photo of Gweniver. If she'd been smiling, and had a hat on, she would have looked just like the picture of Zenna Dare.

BAGNIGGE WELLS TAVERN
and Tea Gardens

IMMENSE ATTRACTION

The public are respectfully informed
that there will be a

Grand
Concert and Ball.

TUESDAY OCTOBER 21ST 1846.

The following professional Ladies and Gentlemen
are already engaged:

Mr. Drew	Miss F Glynne
Miss G. Rivers	Mr. Smith
Miss Dare	Mr. Ashton
Mr. H. Sumner	Mrs. Dutton

SEVERAL OVERTURES

TICKETS SIX-PENCE EACH

The Concert to commence at seven —
the Ball will commence at ten o'clock.

I have a go at Dad at breakfast. Even Steffi and the kids are there but I don't let it stop me. 'Why didn't you tell me more about our family? Did they all come from Cornwall?'

He looks up. 'I'm sure I would have told you that, Jenefer.'

'Well, I don't think you did.'

Dad just sighs. To be fair, he may have told us. Maybe I hadn't been interested, but I sure as hell am now. 'So tell me about Cornwall. I thought you said our family was English.'

He grins at this, toast suspended between his plate and mouth. 'There might be something to be said for genetic memory. That's spoken by a true Cornish woman, if ever I've heard one.'

What on earth is he raving on about? He stops grinning when he sees the frown on my face.

'Jenefer, in reality Cornwall is a county of England, but ethnically, the Cornish have always set themselves apart. You see, they were Celts — there before the English came …'

Incredible. The English were invading even then? Wait until I tell Caleb.

'… now the Cornish are officially recognised as a national minority group.'

'How come you've never said?' I haven't heard him talk about this, I'm sure of it.

'I didn't think you'd be interested. Aunt Dorie knows

more. She belongs to a Cornish Association where they keep up with what's happening over there.'

'So which hostel is Aunt Dorie in?'

'In the Retirement Village in Gawler East. Look, if there's something you want to know, I might be able to help.' Then he smiles. 'It's the house, isn't it? It's so old, it brings the past alive. It's amazing to think our ancestors actually lived and walked in here, spoke across this table. Thanks for the porridge, Mrs Tremayne. I'll be back in after I've fixed the wheel on the dray. Bet they made pasties for lunch.'

Yeah, we think this is old. Caleb's people have been around for 60,000 years. Hamilton's spreading Vegemite even more quietly than usual and Kate's getting interested now. She pipes up, 'Do you know anything about them? Our ancestors?'

'Not much about the original ones, the ones who must have come out and built the house. They were mining people, from Cornwall. All I heard was they lived here in Kapunda, had a cricket team of kids.'

'Is it all written down somewhere? Is it? I'd like to read the story.' Kate again. But she's right. I'd like to read it too. Hamilton's watching, his toast forgotten. Interesting. Hamilton may be quiet but he always eats. Like Sher Khan.

'As far as I know most of the immigrants of those times tried to put their old life behind them.'

'Why did they do that?'

'They knew they'd never return to their homeland again, and to help them adjust and not go mad, I suppose, they didn't teach their kids about it. Just said South Australia was their home now and got on with it.' Sounds very British stiff upper lip. Wonder if they all felt like that?

'Do you know where in Cornwall?' (Checking what I read last night on the back of the envelope)

'Aunt Dorie always said it was Camborne. That was a mining place too and when they started to realise there was a good life over here with copper found in Kapunda, they emigrated.'

I'm starting to feel weird, as though I have no right to a place of my own any more. So I'm of Cornish descent — it's nice to know. But I'm beginning to wonder if Caleb's right about a lot of things and where does that leave me? This isn't really our ancestors' land this house is built on. It could be Caleb's ancestors' for all I know. And if what he's saying is anything to go by, I bet they never got paid for it.

'Why emigrate? Did they ever think their descendants might have liked to stay on their own land?'

'That was just it. They never had land in Cornwall. They'd never get on in life back there. The rich landlords owned it all. The average person made a very small living out of the mines or the sea. Think about how small Cornwall is — it's only the size of Kangaroo Island.' That tiny? It keeps me quiet for a while.

'Jenefer, your great-grandparents were most probably thinking of you three kids when they came.' Hamilton's eyes grow wider and I don't have time to cut in to explain. 'They left everything — family, friends, what they would have called a normal way of life, braved a five-month voyage on a crowded wooden ship that we wouldn't take out in the Gulf — all so their descendants could have the opportunities you have today.'

Guess I'm meant to feel proud about something here, but all I can think about is Caleb, and the box. How does it all fit together? I still want to keep the box a secret for a while, especially since Kate's here and she's like a rabbit colony, all ears, but I have to ask the next question. 'Have you heard of a Zenna Dare?'

Dad shakes his head. 'No. Someone you're doing in History?'

Careful, Kate's watching me; she's so sharp. 'Just heard the name somewhere, that's all.'

It's not until after school and I'm with Caleb that I try to work out some of the confusion. He seems to have a fairly good grip on what he thinks about life and his place in it.

'I have to go to work later so I've got the ute. Want a lift?' Who'd say no? Why did I ever rave about blue eyes? When Caleb's brown eyes go all warm, it feels like they're touching me and I get this urge to jump right into them. But it's the ute I pull myself into and I start straight in about the box.

'It's exciting in one way — I want to find out everything. I mean, it feels good to know something about myself that I didn't know before, because this is about me, isn't it? Not just my great-grandparents or something.' Caleb nods. Then I say it, 'I think I would have been more over the moon a week ago, if I had found the box then.'

Caleb looks at me sharply; even slows down. 'Why's that?'

I find it hard to put into words what's been bothering me for days. 'I feel bad now that they came at all. Maybe I should have been born in Cornwall. People like you could have kept their land and life intact.'

Caleb's shaking his head; I think he mutters a word under his breath that I'm not meant to hear. Then he says something really weird. 'Guilt is not a good basis for a relationship.' *Guilt? Relationship. Whose relationship?*

'What do you mean?'

'I mean, you're sorry about it. That means you want to understand. It's enough.' He's looking at me again. 'There is room for both of us in Kapunda, you know.' He's grinning now as he says Kapunda and I'm not sure if I'm having the mickey taken out of me or not.

'Look, let's stop at the reserve awhile. I'll tell you a story.'

We're near the duck pond and he pulls over. I find out the duck pond is really the Davidson Reserve; used to be a dam and a water stop for bullock drays. It's just as peaceful as when I brought the kids last week. We sit out on the decking, me trailing my fingers in the water, while Caleb tells his story.

'There was once this little girl, five years old, happy, playing with her brothers and sisters.' I grin; he sounds so cute, but my smile soon fades. 'One day a white man came. He chose her and her brother for a special life — to learn the white man's ways. They had the palest skin of that whole mob, you see. Their mum pleaded with him not to take them — she would teach them all she knew and love

49

them more than anyone else ever could, because they were her own, but the white man didn't understand her talk. He thought she didn't have a brain, that she'd soon get over it, or have some more to take their place.

'The little girl was taken to a special school, like a hostel. She was taught lots of things, especially how to clean houses she'd never lived in, and wash clothes she'd never worn. Whenever she drew pictures, ones that she knew were special and reminded her of the stories her mum told, she was smacked for wasting time scribbling. Finally she forgot almost everything — where she came from, even her name. She tried to keep track of where her brother had gone, but it wasn't until she was grown that she saw him again.

'When she was fourteen, she ran away. She didn't know who she was. Her name was Normie now, but it didn't sit right. She still remembered a fire at night and stories and cuddles and the vague warmth of special times. She couldn't find that anywhere. She got into trouble, but no one helped. She couldn't make anyone understand that she just wanted a space somewhere to call her own, one that was meant to be hers. One night she tried to kill herself — she was homeless by then. The weird thing is, it was a Salvation Army officer who found her, in time. Took her home. White do-gooders took her away in the first place — yet another gave her back her life. This one understood. He got her in touch with a Nunga group who helped her start tracing her roots. She's been doing that ever since.'

'Your mum?' I still ask even though I know.

He nods. 'She's still got a pile of baggage from what happened, but every new bit she finds out, she relays on to me, so I'll know who I am. When I tell my kids, they'll know who they are too. They won't have to be like so many of us who have no life, no self-confidence, putting up with people who don't understand why we're like we are.'

I can feel the passion in his tone and it makes my eyes water. Caleb doesn't strike me as having low self-esteem, so I guess his mum's been doing a good job of it.

'And your uncle? She found him?'

Caleb doesn't answer at first. 'Yeah, but he never got over it — being separated like that. They managed to find where they'd been taken from but they couldn't communicate at first with their own people. And their mum had died. With a broken heart, most probably. He was okay in the bush. Would go bush a lot, but it wasn't his own place and he knew it. There was never that spot with his name on it. And there should have been. He just couldn't live in between.' That's all Caleb says, but I can tell his uncle suicided. I don't ask any more; it's too awful. How many people know all this? Do Dad and Steffi? In Australian studies last year I don't remember picking all this up. Too busy dreaming about Ben Walker instead.

Caleb turns to me. 'I told you that because it's only through knowing where she's come from, finding her real family again, that Mum has survived. She doesn't hold a grudge now. That's why it's important for you to find out what's in that box.'

He's moved closer, close enough to hold my hand but he doesn't. 'Honest, Jenefer. I've seen it with our mob. The more they know about themselves, the better they can accept others.' Just the way he's saying it is making the box seem important too. In the light of his mum's story it had begun to pale in comparison.

'Have you told other people this?' Maybe if he has that would explain his acceptance at school, though I've noticed it's only the people who know him well who do accept him, like the guys who play sport. Even Erin has a few reservations. 'Old-fashioned' is one of the surprising phrases she's used in relation to Caleb, though I wouldn't have called it that — more a lack of awareness of little things that cool people think are important. But he shakes his head. 'Not everyone wants to know, Jenefer. And even if we do tell people, it's like seeds on stony ground — only a few take root.'

'Why did you tell me?' I whisper.

His head is down, looking at my hand. I'm staring at the black curls straying past his collar like corkscrews and suddenly I want to reach out, see if they feel springy, but I don't dare. He touches my hand. 'Because I think you'd care.'

'You can't know that.' Alicia fleetingly comes to mind. How does he know I'd be any different? I don't think I am. Surely she'd be upset too if he told her his mum's story. He's still touching my hand. Running his finger down my thumb. It's gentle and feels sharp like electricity at the same time.

'It's just something I can't explain. A feeling I get — a look in someone's eyes. A quick flash on their face that says what they're thinking.' He glances across at me. 'It's not so weird. When you've lived with knowing people mightn't think the best of you, you get to know who will.'

'So you can tell what I'm thinking?' I'm trying to grin, but he's still serious.

'Sometimes.'

I'm getting worried that he's not smiling. Has he caught on that I never understood anything about his people before? That I've lived here all my life; my people have lived here for generations, and I wasn't told? What an excuse. I just never bothered to find out. Does it have to take meeting someone like Caleb before stuff like this makes sense? I'm sitting here staring at his fingers stroking mine. How did I get to know him in such a short time? The things we've shared? The things Caleb's said that I've never heard anyone else say?

'Jenefer,' he says finally, 'your story is important too. Don't ever think it isn't.'

It's night. I'm staring up through my ground-level window where I can see the moon sending its laser beams of pale light. If I half close my eyes I can almost see the faeries sliding down, right into my room. It's incredible what this room has done for me. I still miss my friends from Cedar Rise but I can hardly remember what Ben Walker looks like. Whenever I think of him, Caleb rides through my thoughts like they're trees lining a forest path. It still doesn't stop me feeling like a twig that's dropped off its branch and landed splat in the creek. Amy rang tonight. She told me about her subjects — Classics included, of course — and raved on about how much I'd enjoy it. She was shocked out of her brain that I had no choice in mine, well, not much of a one. She invited me to stay with her for the year. 'It wouldn't be hard, Jenny, and you could go back for holidays.' She sounded as if there couldn't possibly be anything in Kapunda for me. It made me cry after. I tried to explain to her about my room. I stopped at the box, and suddenly realised there's no way right now I could leave that. Nor could I explain what Caleb is like. He has this energy, sort of wild, but he's gentle too. You can see it in his eyes, in his hands. Amy and I used to tell each other everything but I didn't tell her Caleb was a Nunga. I wasn't sure she'd understand.

Tonight I have to force myself to do some homework. There's so much other stuff crowding my mind. If I research Zenna Dare as my History independent study, I can kill two birds with one stone. Now I come to think of it, if I did it all on the web, I could get IT credit too. Even write something up for English. I didn't get away with doing three subjects. Only in special circumstances, I was told. It makes me wonder what special circumstances Caleb has.

At least History is better than what I thought. I would rather have done Classics and it still annoys me but I haven't complained too much lately to Dad. This semester the history is South Australian and it's good for me that Ms East is encouraging us to use local history for research. I've read some of my English novel, an old one by Thomas Hardy about a girl called Tess. Bit depressing so far. She has no control over anything that happens in her life. Worse than being dragged off to Kapunda even.

Now I do what I've been dying to do all day: I open the box again. This time I'm ready. Caleb reckons the box has been left for a reason. I think he's right. No one would leave a box like this filled with personal effects without hoping someone would find it. Otherwise they would have burnt the things. I want to know what Gweniver was like and find out who Zenna Dare was. There's an absurd idea like the beginning phrase of an elusive tune trying to take root in my head but I have to prove something first before I can give it room to develop.

I put the photo of Gweniver in a spare photo frame by my bed. Now she's where she should be where relatives (that's me) can see her. At this point I'm feeling too nostalgic to care about Kate's inquisitive habits. Besides, I can put it in my drawer whenever I go out. Then I take out the leather case of papers. The box has an ink bottle, long ago dried out, and a place to put the pen. Must have been a dip pen, that long ago. When the lid lifts up there's a blotter on the inside of the lid and a surface to write on. In a hollow space under this are the papers. They're not in order, and I can tell it's going to take too long to work out what comes first; they're not all dated. Some are just poems, some look like letters, or journal writing on sheets of paper. Some of the paper looks like it was ripped out of a book to be written on. The ones torn in pieces will have to be left for last. The ink is faded so I sit close to the light. It's hard to decipher and the form of the letters is different from mine. Guess I'll just read what comes — a bit whenever I can — late at night when everyone's in bed. It won't give me much time, but there's no other way to keep it secret.

The first thing I notice is how sad my great-grandmother is. Oops, 1845 — she can't just be my great-grandmother. How many 'greats' back to 1845? I work it out on a pad. If everyone had most of their kids by thirty-five, and Great-aunt Dorie is my grandparents' generation, then Gweniver is my great-great-great-grandmother. Totally incredible. What a mouthful! From now on 'triple-great-grandmother' will have to do.

> O rose thou art sick.
> The invisible worm
> That flies in the night
> In the howling storm
> Has found out thy bed
> Of crimson joy;
> And his dark secret love
> Does thy life destroy.

This is written out in ink and says William Blake on the bottom. Why did she collect such sad poems? I smooth out one of the pages and start to work out what it says.

GWENIVER

CAMBORNE, CORNWALL, 1845

Sweet rose, fair flower, untimely pluckt, soon faded,
Pluckt in the bud and faded in the spring!
Bright orient pearl, alack, too timely shaded!
Fair creature, kill'd too soon by death's sharp sting!
  Like a green plum that hangs upon a tree
  And falls through wind before the fall should be.

'The Passionate Pilgrim',
William Shakespeare 1564–1616

How I have been plucked. I am the one who should be dead. If only I could turn back the sun's rising, back to the heady joys and simple pleasures of childhood. Learning the lute at grandmother's knee; singing those simple songs 'Trelawny' and 'Pretty Little Mermaid'. What a memory I had for words. Grandmama would sing a song once and then I could remember it the next day. Nor did it take me long to learn the lute, even though I quailed when I first counted all those strings. Mama was always so pleased when I played, though Da would grumble. 'Look 'ere,' he would say, 'the child should be learnin' to make pasties.' But I already knew how to make pasties, how to make the onions stretch when there was no meat. Lute playing was more of a challenge.

Gladys would go on at me if ever I ran and washed my hands between putting loaves in the oven, just so I could play and sing. Not even sweet Mary seemed to understand the force that drove me like Da's shirt flying in the northern wind. I could no more stop singing than that shirt could stop flapping. We all went to school. Mama saw to that; another thing Da grumbled about when his friends' daughters were bal maidens, preparing the ore, while we learnt our letters and embroidery. But Mama was adamant, 'No daughters o' mine will be missin' out on fine chances because of a lack of "edication".' I never realised they both worked harder because of it, until Clarice and Gladys took 'positions'.

Perhaps Mama's educational idea was because we were not as beautiful as some. I can remember Grandmama, before she died, telling Mama that with a face like hers, Annie Trengove would never need to go to school. I was glad I was ugly enough for school, then. Once I realised I could read, I knew anything was possible. No matter we never heard the sound of a bird singing for the constant thump of the mine engine, I could visit other worlds, hear their birds sing in books. I soon learnt that the musical tongue my parents spoke was not the language of school. The shame of not knowing the proper words gradually passed as I practised saying my aitches where I should and removing them where they should not be; saying 'you' instead of 'ee'. Words, English words, were magical and I respected them for the power they held.

Yet even with the reading, many things were not explained. We learned the important things as time went by, until suddenly one was grown up and one miraculously knew what to do. That is how I understood life. I know now I was naive, but that day when Mr. Drew was passing through Camborne, I was sixteen and I knew all there was to know. Da still had not walked home from the mine, and I had escaped for a short while with the lute. In a field at Pen Ponds I was, playing and singing some simple song, 'Maggie May', most like. I saw the young gentleman pass by; he barely hesitated. How much he had heard before he came into sight I could not tell. But I knew it would not do to be seen idling away minutes with a lute so I stopped playing at once and hurried the quarter-mile back to the cottage.

It was later that it all happened. The March Fair, a celebration on the common; Da said we could all go. The first Friday of March was always a holiday for the mine. Perhaps we had St Piran to thank for that. Clarice and Gladys fussed over the little ones; Mary and I were left to ourselves to get ready. I was looking forward to the fiddlers and dancers, the pedlars with things to sell we had never seen before. When we arrived, the dancing had already started on the green and we quickly joined in. The young gentleman was there too in his blue dress coat and narrow breeches. I had never seen him before he passed the field, but here he was in front of me, dancing, with almost a smile curling on his lips. I tried not to notice and I did not smile back for we had not been introduced.

Soon it was announced there was to be a prize given. The sweetest song from a young lady would win her lessons with a singing master in Penzance. There had always been music booths at fairs but I had never sung in them before. I closed my eyes with the pain of it. Singing lessons. Did I dare hope? A desperate fluttering started up in my middle; I could hardly speak clearly when I sought out my mother.

'May I, Mama? Sing in this public place?'

My mother was a bumble bee that had just flown into a field of bluebells. 'Of course, child. Your one chance, this may be.' I was touched. With the Cornish knack of putting first in the sentence what was most important, my mother had shown me she knew what lay so heavily on my heart.

'And Da?'

'Later. To 'un I will be explainin'.' I felt the fear then mixed in with the other trembling. Perhaps this was not the right time? Da would not approve, I knew that, but Mama pushed me from behind. 'Get on with 'ee, your grandmama didn't die leavin' 'ee that lute and voice so 'ee be doin' nothin' with 'em.'

When I went to the Master of Ceremonies to register, the young gentleman was sitting at the table writing down all the names. He looked up as I came close; his eyebrows rose and I knew he recognised me, perhaps even from the field in Pen Ponds. So close he did not seem as young as I first thought. I felt that unreasonable lurch in my innards again, but I explained it away as excitement.

Agonising it was, waiting for my turn. Some girls even sang 'Trelawny'. I had realised by now that it was the gentleman who would be choosing; he listened intently to every song, nodded, but never completely smiled. He did not look like the type of man to be moved by Cornwall's folk tunes. I chose 'Lamorna', a more worldly type of song to impress a gentleman from Penzance. Penzance. He may as well be from London.

When it was finally my turn, I sang well enough after the first few words; perhaps not quite as well as I could in the field. It was terribly disconcerting having so many hear me who were only used to seeing me sing Wesley's tunes in Chapel. When all had finished, the gentleman looked down at his paper and wrote a name. Looking back now, 'tis easy to see he decided too quickly. But I did not notice that then, no one did, not even Da, who seemed resigned to be pleased for me after all.

'Though I doubt 'ee'll be able to make a living from singin', child. Best take good note of what the teacher tells 'ee, so 'ee can teach it 'eeself one day.'

There was only a night to say goodbye. I was to travel with Mrs. Moyle who was to get me settled into a boarding house. Penzance was almost fifteen miles away; I would miss the Whit-Monday picnic, even Midsummer. *Why, I might not be home again before Christmas.*

I can still remember that song I sang at the fair:

This song I'll sing to you —
It's about a maiden fair,
I met the other evening
At the corner of the square;
She'd a dark and roving eye
And her hair was covered over,
And we roved all night
In the pale moonlight
Away down to Lamorna.

JENEFER

I have to see Great-aunt Dorie. Nothing seems quite so important any more as Zenna Dare or my triple-great-grandmother. Nor have I told Dad about the box. I just don't want to lose it — it could end up in the Kapunda museum. Or, at best, in the lounge where Kate will find out all its secrets, and I feel like I need to know more before I can cope with that invasion. I can almost understand what Caleb talks about as sacred things in his culture.

Ms East approved this as a local research project for my independent History assignment. I'll call it *Zenna Dare*. I just hope my instincts aren't wrong and there actually is something to research. English — I sure would have written the end of *Tess of the d'Urbervilles* differently from Thomas Hardy. But then, I didn't live in the society he lived in. Were people all that much different? Thomas Hardy is Mr Mayes's passion. There was no chance for Tess to redeem herself, he reckons. It's so unfair; the first guy was a sleaze date-raping her like that and Angel Clare was such a hypocrite. But she couldn't see any of it coming. 'One day she was pink and flawless, the next tragical.' At least Hardy tries to make the reader think about it, like was 'once lost always lost' really true of chastity? 'Is maidenhood' (the ancient word for virginity, would you believe) 'the only part of the body denied healing power?' In a case like poor old Tess, it certainly wasn't for a lack of wishing it back. At least I'm getting ideas for the first essay.

The kitchen is too quiet for Saturday when I get up there. Well, not quite: Hamilton is sniffing. I thought he'd be happy, going down to the shops with Steffi and Kate.

Caleb's taking me to the home where Aunt Dorie lives. For once he's not working at the farm. It feels like a date. Kate wanted to come too. Dad thought that would be a good rest for Steffi, but I put my foot down. I can, when there's something I want badly enough. Steffi came to my rescue; don't know if she truly needed to take Kate for school shoes or if she thought I needed what she calls a 'lift'. It placated Kate at least and Hamilton gets to go too.

I ruffle Hamilton's hair a bit. 'So what's wrong?' What usually bothers a seven-year-old? A lost toy? A friend doesn't like him anymore? That'd get fixed up the next day, wouldn't it? But Kate answers for him. 'It's Sher Khan.' She doesn't sound upset so I don't catch on at first. Then I see Steffi give her a warning glance, just as Kate opens her mouth. She shuts it again.

'He's sick.' I hardly hear Hamilton's mumble and I give Steffi a questioning glance. She shrugs. 'Not much you can do with little rabbits.' She says it low but Hamilton must have heard — he runs back to his room. At this point I hear the ute round the back and Caleb comes to the kitchen door, ready to take me to Gawler. Just like I did, he senses the atmosphere in the room.

'It's Hamilton's rabbit,' I say and Caleb looks as though he wants to see, so I take him down the hall to Hamilton's room. 'He calls it Sher Khan,' I add and grin at Caleb's raised eyebrows. 'Quite a name for a miniature rabbit, eh?'

Hamilton is sitting by the cage, his back to the doorway.

'Sher Khan not too good, mate?'

Hamilton just shakes his head and stares into the cage. The rabbit doesn't look flash either. It's breathing funny and looks distinctly glassy-eyed. Poor Hamilton. I'm wondering if we can buy another one in Kapunda, when Caleb gets all business-like.

'Go and see if your mum's got some pineapple in the fridge, mate.' Hamilton doesn't need to be asked twice; he runs to the kitchen. The look on his face concerns me though, like Caleb's come to save the day. What if he can't? And pineapple? I'm still wondering about that when Hamilton brings some in.

'Just give him a bit, mate.'

'What will pineapple do?'

'Help get rid of the hair ball.'

'Hairball?'

'Rabbits get them like cats do but they can't vomit them up like cats.'

Incredible. How does he know so much? He sees the look on my face and grins. 'I have done Ag Science since Year 8. I should have picked up something by now.' Then he turns back to Hamilton. 'He should have fresh hay every day, mate. I'll bring some when I go out to the farm tomorrow.'

Hamilton's hesitant, hopeful. 'You think he'll be okay?'

'Sure he will. But he wouldn't be if you hadn't noticed. The hay will help pass the fur through his digestive system. You could brush him some too. Don't worry now.' And what Hamilton does then, I haven't seen him do before, not to anyone other than Dad. He runs at Caleb full pelt, almost knocks him off balance and buries his face in his middle. What Caleb does next will determine whether he has a friend for life or not. I needn't worry. Caleb doesn't hesitate. He picks Hamilton up and walks him to the window. Then he whispers something in Hamilton's ear and I see the kid nodding. Caleb seems totally at ease as though he's lived around kids forever but I know he's the youngest in his family. Then I notice Kate. The look on her face shocks me. Kate always has been one for strong emotion — whatever it is — but what could cause the screwed-up redness that looks like jealousy? Pique that Hamilton's getting attention? Or is it Caleb? He turns then. Kate and I both smile but Kate's eyes still look glassy and hard. The moment passes; Caleb grins at Kate, tells a joke on the way to the kitchen. Then we're out of there.

'So cool for you to take me,' I say to Caleb on the way.

'Hey, no problem.' It feels good that he understands. He's been through all this family stuff with his mum and miraculously isn't bored by it. Somehow, his mother has instilled a sense of 'before' in Caleb and imparted the importance of it. Can't think of any of my friends from

Cedar Rise who'd be remotely interested, although Sokha may have. Certainly not Amy. We never talked about stuff like this. I remember Kate then and try not to feel guilty; maybe she wanted to come. Yet I wasn't interested in family at ten. Why should she be?

Great-aunt Dorie isn't quite as I remember her from Grandad's funeral. He was my last real grandparent. Now I have only Steffi's set, not really mine.

'Hello, dear.' Aunt Dorie knows me, even though she looks a little tattered round the edges. Her hair's just been curled and coloured with grandma blue. From the doorway I can smell the hairspray attacking the atmosphere.

'You look so much like your mother now, dear.' I smile politely, knowing I don't at all until I realise she means my real mum — the one I don't remember. She was a Kapunda girl too, Nicky Batten. She knew Dad in the same cattle king high school. I wonder if they ever sat on the grass near the 1920s statue or walked down the street feeling like I do when Caleb comes with me. I fight to keep my mind on the job at hand; Caleb's stayed in the cafeteria, at least. Another one of those things I 'should do by myself'. I take out the photo of Gweniver, and hand it to Aunt Dorie.

'I found this in the house, Aunt Dorie.' Some instinct stops me telling her about the box. 'Do you recognise her?'

She holds the photo up to the light of the window behind her. 'This looks like Gweniver Tremayne. Bit young, though.' She turns it over. 'Gweniver Rundle, 1845. So that was her maiden name.' Aunt Dorie gives me a look that's hard to read. 'This is very old, Jenefer. Photography wasn't popular until later. Only rich people could afford it. Funny, I never thought they were —' Her voice fades and I sit down close to her to prompt her. 'What were they?'

'Miners, we always thought. Came out to Kapunda when the copper was found.' She pushes herself up out of the chair and shuffles over to a dresser. A few drawers get opened and shut until she pulls out a tin box and finds what she's looking for. She brings it back — a photo. It's a much older Gweniver, with hair piled up on both sides of her head and a million kids arranged straight-faced around her. I count the kids — eight. Standing behind them is a man — tall, dark hair, grey on his temples.

'He's a babe,' I say and Aunt Dorie actually twinkles. 'Your great-great-great grandfather, Redvers Tremayne. Yes, he is rather dashing, isn't he? Bet he was one for the ladies with looks like that.' I stare harder. The square high collar almost frames his chin. There's a ghost of a smile; two little lines at the right corner of his mouth give him away. And the look in his eyes — it's not the deadpan look so many old photos have. It's like he can really see me and wants to say hello. Suddenly something flops inside me. Tears are springing to the back of my eyes, my nose is burning trying not to let it show. I can't explain what I'm feeling, I only wish I knew him, and Gweniver. I can just imagine the look Caleb would have on his face if he were here and I begin to understand why people like Caleb's mum spend so much time finding out about their ancestors.

'They look really nice.' It's a lame statement considering what's forcing its way through my veins, my head, my heart. If only they could talk to me. 'Do you know anything, Aunt Dorie? About them?'

'Only that they settled in Kapunda. He was the one who built the house.'

'What about before?'

'They came from Camborne. We don't know much. I had a few books and letters from my father, Albert. The family Bible.'

I smell progress. 'The family Bible?'

'Emily has that, but I could get her to bring it when she comes next.'

'Yes, please.' Right now anything sounds helpful and I think she senses my impatience.

'She doesn't get here often, of course. There's nothing more in there, just the dates when the children were born and one died. The wedding too. In the 1850s I think it was. But you can find out yourself.'

I feel like a drug-sniffer dog. 'Really?'

'The library has all sorts of things nowadays if you're interested.' Then she looks at me with a half-smile. The expression in her eyes is shrewd but kind. 'Why are you interested?'

I mumble something about knowing who I am, where I come from; anything I can think of that doesn't involve the word 'box'.

Just before I go, I produce the photo of Zenna Dare.

'Do you know who this is?'

She looks at it, adjusts her multi-focals, glances back at the one of Gweniver and Redvers. 'No, never seen this before. But it does have a likeness to the younger version of Gweniver, doesn't it? How strange.' My sentiments exactly.

'Is there any way they could be related?' I don't dare say what I seriously wish.

'I shouldn't think so. Our people were ordinary mining folk from Cornwall. The English used to look down on such people. This Miss Zenna Dare must have been someone special, a society person maybe, with a dress like that. Couldn't be any connection.'

Then I show her the letter-card with *Dear Zenna* on it. She reads it all through, then looks at it, confused. 'Maybe Zenna Dare was someone she admired. Maybe Gweniver looked like her, so for a lark her young man called her Zenna. 'R' for Redvers, I suppose. A pet name, Jenefer?'

I nod slowly. She's most probably right; but the sleuth in me rebels. It sounds so ordinary. And why was it all in a secret room in a cleverly crafted trick box? I try again.

'Don't you think there might have been more to it? Was nothing said at all? Did your father ever mention anything? Or your aunts? Wasn't there anything?' I've gone too far. A shadow passes over Aunt Dorie's face. I see it and stop, but not soon enough. It could be just my tone she doesn't like. She breathes in. It's too long, and it takes a while to expel it all. Then …

'Jenefer,' she starts, 'whatever it was, it is in the past.

I'm sure it's nothing. Something quite innocent, but whatever it was, it was their business alone.' She pauses but not long enough for me to get a word in. 'It's one thing to find out who our forebears are and where they come from — it brings a certain satisfaction — but to want to know personal details about their lives is nothing short of morbid. Really, Jenefer, don't think any more about this.'

My mind is racing alongside hers; what if something's meant to be known but for some reason it doesn't get passed on? Look at Caleb's family. They never knew who they were because his mum was taken away from her family and she never found out in the proper way. Now she has to rely on records people may have kept. Me too, I guess. Aunt Dorie keeps on.

'If there was anything meant to be known, it would have been handed down, so we could all know. It's either nothing, or it was meant to stay hidden —' She couldn't know just how hidden the box was. I can never tell her about it now. She'd get Dad to seal up the room again with the box in it, before I got to find out anything.

One thing I know as I stand up to leave. Aunt Dorie's words have solidified what's been in melt-down in my head the last few weeks — that I'm meant to find out. I have to know and it's not just for me. At least Aunt Dorie lets me take the family photo to get a copy.

'Dyw genes,' she says, just before I close the door.

'Pardon?'

'It's Kernewek for goodbye, dear. They're reviving the

Cornish language.' I smile and try to say it back. Guess she must care about the culture if she's learnt the old language.

Caleb joins me but he doesn't ask me anything, just waits. I appreciate that. My head's swirling like bath water being let out; I just hope I catch what I'm meant to, before it all gets sucked down the black hole.

'Caleb, just one stop before we go home, please?'

'OK. Then I'm shouting you lunch. Where're we headed?'

'The library.'

The Gawler Library has been caught in a time warp, all heavy, old, brown wood smelling like another age, with dark green and maroon leather-bound books; it's like walking back a century and a half. *Had any of my ancestors walked on this floor?* It's that sort of place — makes you think impossible things. Soon I have a cloth-bound green book in my hand, *Arrivals to South Australia*. I look up 'Rundle' but there's no entry for Gweniver. I try 'Tremayne'; there are quite a few but I find the right one:

> *TREMAYNE Arthur b: 1799 Gwennap CON*
> *ENG d:1859 Kapunda SA arr. John 1840 occ:*
> *miner res: Kapunda*
> *m: Elizabeth nee Moyle 1820 Gwp CON ENG*
> *chn: Susannah (1823–1871) Redvers (1825–*
> *1890) Maria (1826) Elizabeth (1827–1851)*
> *Jane (1830-1893) John (1832–1887) Henry*
> *(1835–1840).*

My triple-great-grandfather in a book! I stare at it for a while, then remember it still doesn't tell me about Gweniver. I keep looking; there are more Tremaynes — columns of them: Albert, Thomas, William, and finally I see mine again.

> *TREMAYNE Redvers b: 1825, Gwennap CON ENG d: 1890 Kapunda, arr: 1840 JOHN occ: miner, farmer, res: Kapunda rel: BC m 1852 Kapunda SA Gweniver nee RUNDLE par: John Rundle and Mary Batten b 15.5.1828 Camborne, CON, ENG, arr: 1849 JOHN WOODALL chn: Emmelene (1853–1894), Mary-Jayne (1854–1874), Percy (1855-1901), Nathan (1855-1912), Thomas (1857–1930), Rebekah (1859–1860), John (1860–1885), William (1862–1941), Elliot (1863–1923).*

I stare at the page, hardly believing all this information is here and none of us knew. *Gweniver Rundle arr 1849.* So Gweniver came as a single woman; she must have married here, not in Cornwall, like Dad and Aunt Dorie think. I look up 'Dare'. It's an English name and there are pages of them, but I can't find Zenna's name.

'Any luck?' Caleb's peering over my shoulder.

'Just look at all this stuff. I can't find Zenna Dare, though. I wonder if she came out with Gweniver. Like two single ladies together. Can't imagine a girl coming out alone.' That elusive tune starts winding up in my head again but I put the damper pedal down fast. I don't dare give it room yet. 'Gweniver was only twenty-one when she came.' I turn round to look at Caleb, to see if he's listening and he's grinning so wide it's almost audible.

'What?'

'You sound just like my mum. She gets excited too, but in a quiet sort of way. Though she doesn't find out as much in one spot like this.'

We leave the library armed with photocopies of the Tremayne pages of the register of South Australian immigrants.

Much later, I go down to the Kapunda library and ask for the marriage certificates for 1852. 'So sorry,' the librarian says, 'but only records since 1856 are kept here. The rest are on CD or digitised in the Mortlock library.'

'Mortlock?'

'In the city; part of the State Library on North Terrace.'

I wonder if Caleb would like a date in the city one Saturday. Soon.

GWENIVER

Go, lovely rose,
Tell her that wastes her time and me,
That now she knows,
When I resemble her to thee,
How sweet and fair she seems to be.

'Song', Edmund Waller 1606–1687

Five months, two weeks and three days on a ship does not bear thinking about once it is over. The captain seemed pleased at the end that only nine people had died and most of them babes under two. It has been the only time I have been thankful that I shall not have a family of my own.

Will was there in Port Adelaide to meet me. This is such a sparse, hot and vast land. If I did not know I had no hope of a normal life behind me, I think I should lose heart and immediately return home. It is late November and the temperature must be upwards of 100 degrees. Surely we were never meant to live in a place such as this. Wherever one looks there is brown, and the hills are purple, while everything is covered with a shimmery haze. It could not be called pretty at all.

Adelaide is not unlike a village at home, except for the

lack of beautiful old churches and spires. There was a great bustling of bullock drays and carts, and a lot of rough-looking fellows riding about on splendid horses. At least there are no beggars. The house where we rested belongs to a friend of Will's. They came in 1839 when Adelaide was little more than a gypsy camp. I cannot imagine anything more primitive than what everyone seems proud of now. Yet become used to it I must; the distance from my family has much more than ten thousand miles to do with it.

At eleven the next morning we took the mail cart north to Kapunda. There were eight of us on board this vehicle covered with canvas that I'm sure must have been built to carry only five. One lady had a bonnet box that became hideously crushed on the way. At least we were driven by a cheery person by name of Jemmy Chambers. He called the cart a trap but I think he rather overstated his outfit. Will said Mr. Chambers was a reckless whip and I believe him, for every jolt nearly unseated us all and was a cause for remark. Soon all the passengers were amiably talking. Most unlike travel in Cornwall. The dust was intolerable yet no one was cross with Mr. Chambers for the brisk ride since he was such an amusing man.

Just as we were descending a gully and scaling the bank of a river (with no water, I was astonished to see) an accident occurred. Even Mr. Chambers' confidence could not stop a pole breaking. While we women alighted and fanned ourselves in the heat, Mr. Chambers borrowed a sapling from a neighbouring fence and substituted it for the original pole. Some of the men passengers, Will included, gave assistance. I was sure the wheels of the cart would fall off as well, with the depth of the holes in the road. By the time we reached a place called The Old Spot Inn, I was thankful to rest. My back felt as though all the bones had been rearranged in a most disagreeable design.

The next day at six in the morning we made off for Kapunda. I was upset to find the mail cart would return to Adelaide and we were obliged to continue the journey in a spring cart bound for Burra Burra with no protection at all from the sun and the dust. It was little better than the bullock drays I saw on the road the day before. The horses were inferior too and I am sure one was lame, while the driver used his whip overmuch. It is so much further than anyone would travel in Cornwall, yet because of the wide open spaces the journey did not seem long. In Cornwall, there's a village at almost every mile, with the usual slowing down and change of pace before and afterwards. But here, the horses can get up a good gallop as there is nothing to stop them. Except the bushrangers or marauding blacks, they say.

Just before we reached Kapunda we saw some of the native people. The women were naked except for a skin cape from an animal called an opossum, Will said. With them was a man who had a long bone driven through his nose. They put me in a state of disquiet for the remainder of the journey until I glimpsed Mary waiting for us, shading her face from the sun.

Emily and little George are darlings. With much embarrassment, Emily presented me with a fine straw hat. Even though we were all allowed only one trunk per family on the boat I was able to bring presents for them all. How large families managed I shall never know. I brought tea for Mary since it is so expensive here. Emily loves her new lace-up boots and George has started playing his tin whistle already. I remarked to Mary how much George resembles our brother Georgie and we both fell quiet. It was a terrible way to die, falling down the shaft like that. A thousand feet, Da said.

Dear Mary has not alluded to my previous life and nor shall I. It is now behind me. I am fortunate to be able to start afresh where no one knows me. Mary and Will have a cottage in North Kapunda, agreeably situated on rising ground. It has two rooms and is made of slabs of wood plastered over with mud and straw. Will says the thatched roof helps to lessen the heat and soon he will start work on another room made of stone.

Kapunda is much like a mining town at home with the noise and dust. No one has planted a garden, and even the trees are sparse after the cutting of them for the mine. Mary gets her water from a barrel submerged at the back of the cottage, but Will has to cart it from the lower dam where the bullock drays and carts stop. All the rooms are built on the ground floor; there is no upstairs as in Cornwall. Will says it is because there is enough land here for folk to spread out. He is the first man to own this land that the cottage is built upon. There are eighty acres; the Crown allowed him to buy it for one pound an acre. He has bought it with the help of another man, William Hawke. He and his wife Susan also have a cottage on it not far away. They are all fast friends. I have never seen so much land owned by two people before but Will assures me the land was unused when copper was found at Kapunda.

Will has whitewashed the cottage to keep it cooler. Even so, I find it difficult to sleep at night for the heat and mosquitoes. Not only mosquitoes but ants, fleas and all sorts of vermin abound, even snakes!

I have started a letter to Gladys to say I arrived safely, but perhaps it is best not to send it. Everyone was so cross when I left; I doubt if Gladys would even read it. Better they forget just as I shall endeavour to do.

JENEFER

I can hear this snuffy, muffled noise coming from Dad and Steffi's room. It's not either of the kids; Dad took them to Dutton Park to watch the cricket. Steffi must have thought I went too. I would have but I really do have too much study to do. I poke my head in.

'Mum? What's wrong?' She sees me and tries to dry up her face. Tissues fly as she rips fresh ones out of the box.

'It's nothing, Jenefer.' The mumble doesn't fool me. 'I'm fine.' She's nodding her head, trying to act like her face is not a squashed tomato.

'No. Really — you can tell me.' I sit down beside her, worried. I can't remember seeing her cry, not gut-felt like this. A tingle starts up behind my nose in sympathy.

'I can't find a job.'

I make a suggestion even while I'm thinking this can't be the real reason. 'The library?'

'Even the volunteers down there have degree in Information Studies. There's an army of them.' She's trying to smile between shudders. 'Everything's either voluntary or filled to the brim all over town.' I grin too as she makes the town sound as if it has more than 4000 people.

'Why don't you start the business you've wanted to?'

'Takes money.'

'What about Auntie Joy? She got a small business grant. You're just as clever and creative. Steffi, you could do anything. Honest. And both the kids are at school now.' With satisfaction, I see her eyes start to gleam with something more than tears.

'I've always wanted to sell my own crafts, restore old things ...'

'Now you can.'

'But I should pull my weight. Your father —'

'You will be when you start selling. What about sheep farmers? They only make money when they sell the wool. They work for nothing the rest of the time. And writers, artists — they only make their money when something sells.' Amazing how roles can get suddenly skew-whiff. Usually Steffi is telling me the encouraging stuff.

Steffi tries another watery smile. 'If even then.' She sighs. 'I suppose I should take a risk. Your father would respect that. It's just that I've tried so hard to fit in. Your father is so happy here and I can't tell him I'm not —' She stops suddenly as if she's said too much, and I'm quiet.

If it weren't for my room and the box and for Caleb, I'd be feeling the same. I came here missing Cedar Rise, my friends, Ben, just knowing I'd hate it. Hoping Sokha or Amy would ask me for weekends. And now? There's Caleb — nothing's been said, but there's that expectation of what may be around the corner. And the box. Its contents constantly fill my imagination. It sure seems to take the edge off feeling depressed about Cedar Rise. And suddenly I make another of my snap decisions.

'You want to see something?'

And I lead her down to my room.

When she sees the box, she draws in breath and buckles suddenly onto my bed. 'What is it?'

'It's like a time capsule. Though I don't think it's meant to be. It's Gweniver Tremayne's.'

Steffi raises wide eyes to mine. 'You mean —?' I nod. 'Have you told your father?'

I hesitate. 'Not yet. Mum —?' But she seems to understand, just bends down to the box. Then she looks up again 'Sometime though, he'll need to know.' Her eyebrows are curled like a question mark and I nod again.

'I want to find out more first. I feel like I'm getting to know Gweniver. She's written some things — letters, poems she's copied out or written from memory. There are pages, out of a journal I think, but they're all jumbled up and it's hard to read. I can't explain it. At the moment it's personal to her and yet it's still mine.' I don't mention the word sacred. 'I just need to know more, before —'

'Before the hungry sharks get in on the kill?'

I stop, amazed at the accurate assessment of Dad and Kate's personalities. 'You agree with me, then?'

She nods now. 'For a while. Do you need any help?'

'Not really. You know when I saw Aunt Dorie?' Steffi just nods; she's running her hand over the roof, like I did.

And Caleb. 'She basically warned me off the whole thing.'

'She knows?'

'Not about the box, but I showed her photos, one of Gweniver — it must have been taken in Cornwall. And of Zenna Dare.' I try to say it lightly, don't let on that every time I say her name it's like I hear a phantom tune in my head, trying to make itself known.

Steffi looks up at that. 'Zenna Dare? So that's why you were asking all those questions. Did Dorie know anything?'

'Not about Zenna Dare. Gweniver, of course, and she got all pensive about how early the photo was.'

'What's early?'

'1845.'

Steffi almost whistles. 'A daguerreotype.' My face must be screwed up (I tend to do that when I don't understand) for she explains, 'It's a sort of photo they did before the 1850s. Expensive.'

I get it out to show her. 'That's what Aunt Dorie said: expensive. And when I asked her about Zenna Dare, she basically told me to mind my own business. Mum, you do understand, don't you? I'm afraid Dad will be like Aunt Dorie, or at the very least, take the box off me, or try and work it out himself. I can just imagine him carting it off to some library resource person and getting them to find out who Zenna Dare was. Where's the fun in that?' Even to Steffi I can't explain how it's more than fun, a quest almost — the 'near sacredness' of the box — that only someone like Caleb would understand.

Steffi's quiet. Then, 'I won't tell. Yet. But I'll ask you first if I think it's necessary. Okay?' That's fair.

I pull out the letter case and show Steffi a piece of paper. 'See? It's all like this. Like she ripped the pages out, maybe to burn, then thought better of it. Every time I look at them I get new ideas of why they're like this. See, some are even ripped in pieces. It's hard to read anyway, so I'm typing them up, one at a time. Trying to put dates on them and where I think it happened, according to things she's written before. The ones in pieces I'll be able to work out when the rest are done.'

'That's quite a job.' I can tell what Steffi's thinking: when will I ever do any homework?

'Don't worry. I'm using it for my assignments.' I don't miss her approving grin. She's totally forgotten about feeling rotten. 'See, read this one. I just typed it up.' She takes it from me and reads it aloud:

Kapunda, 1849

Have just met a man called Redvers Tremayne. Tall for a Cornishman. He came from Gwennap, as a child, with his parents in 1840. They have lived here in Kapunda since the mine opened five years ago. He doesn't seem overly pretentious at all; he wore simple black trousers and a frock coat. Nor did he use a top hat, just a broad-

brimmed hat. Sensible in this heat. Mary tells me he
works in the mine, but he was the lay preacher today at
chapel, and I must say the passion in his tone stirred me,
and not only the part that was meant to be stirred, either.
There is no hope for such as I, of course. A man like
that will naturally be put off if he were to learn of my
background.

'Amazing. Imagine finding something like this.' She's glancing at the box, at me and back to the A4 paper in her hand, and I can tell what's going through her mind: treasure. I have found a treasure. 'What on earth does she mean by "background"?'

'No idea.'

'And the rose? You did that?'

'She seems to like roses. Most of the poems I've seen so far are about them. Sad, though.'

'And she mentions Zenna Dare?'

My spirits drop slightly. 'Not that I know of yet. I've tried Zenna Dare on the web but nothing's come up except *Zenna's Furnishings* and a dentist who does crowns.' Steffi laughs. It's a great sound.

'Have you tried an advanced search?'

A hope re-stirs in me.

'You try it. And don't forget to click on *exact phrase* in advanced search or you'll end up with seventy thousand hits about daredevils —'

'— or Zenna's furnishings!' I leave Steffi with the box

and scoot across the slate floor to the twin underground room. I throw on the power, enter the password and connect to the 'net. So glad the kids are out. I do what Steffi suggested: I click on advanced search and select exact phrase. This time when I type in 'Zenna Dare', it should be different. It is. Five hits. A few about the same site, 'Ross's World of Photographs'. I click on one — and there she is. *Zenna Dare 1847*. She's standing in a snow scene in a fur coat, hand muffs and hat, her head on one side, smiling at me. I click on another. There she is again. *Zenna Dare 1848*. This time she's standing on the side, looking back at me. A long dress trails around her, her hair is long and dark, half done up, half hanging down. There's nothing to say who she is, what she did. I try other pages on the site — nothing. There's a space to buy the photographs for fifteen US dollars each. So much. Because they're so old? I find Ross's contact details and send an e-mail:

Dear Ross
I've seen the photos of Zenna Dare for sale on your site. I have one too that I found in my great-great-great-grandmother's papers but I can't seem to find any information about her. Do you have any information about Zenna Dare?
Thank you, Jenefer Tremayne.

I print out the photos. Then I click onto the next address. It's a genealogy site — all full of Dares. Can't find Zenna, though. In frustration I backtrack and click on another URL. This one's about British Theatre. With excitement I click the activated address and I groan. 'URL unavailable'.

I try another: 'Nineteenth Century English Stage'. This one looks promising — maybe she was an actress. But soon I'm almost ready to pack it in. I can't find Zenna's name anywhere. In desperation I hit the 'Find' button and enter 'Zenna Dare', and yes! Here she is again. Her name highlighted, fifteen pages into the document. I would never have found it just by scrolling through. I start reading, but the early flush of excitement soon turns to disappointment. *With Zenna Dare as the ugly sister.* That's it? I scroll back. Nothing else about her at all. Then I find the blue activated words, *La Cenerentola*. It has to be the name of the play. Ugly sister. Cinderella? I hit it but it takes its time. It's like the computer is conspiring against me and I prepare myself for another 'URL unavailable'.

Then colour flicks onto the screen and I know I'm on Zenna's trail at last.

LA CENERENTOLA

THEATRE ROYAL, COVENT GARDEN
Music by Rossini.
Adapted and Arranged by Rophino Lacy.

The first performance of Lacy's pantomime, with its adaptation of Rossini's music, took place on Tuesday, August 14, 1846, at the Theatre Royal, Covent Garden.

The Director was Mr. Rophino Lacy. Stage Director, Mr. Farley. The cast included J. Wood as Prince Felix, Mr. Drew as the

Baron, Miss Ginny Rivers as Cinderella, and Miss Dare and Miss Glynne as Clorinda and Thisbe, the ugly sisters.

The play opened with a faeries' haunt, a romantic scene surrounded by bowers of roses in the midst of which rises a sparkling fountain. A broad lake is seen in the distance, shut in by mountains which stretch to the horizon, and over them the sun is rising. During the overture numerous Sylphs and Faeries enter, forming a dance around the fountain to the chorus, "While Sunbeams Are Glancing". The Faery Queen enters in a swan car to announce her decision to marry the prince to Cinderella. He is the one she has been watching for so as to facilitate his meeting with Cinderella/Angelina, a woman of true virtue.

The play is indeed a statement on human values, an example of how persons of quality can treat the lower orders. The father, rather than a stepmother, is the villain. Mr. Drew shows an excellent performance as the wicked baron who disowns his daughter, and Miss Rivers is convincing as Cinderella. However, one's attention is immediately drawn to the ugly sister, Clorinda, played by Miss Dare, a new face to theatre.

Cinderella, Clorinda and Thisbe sing the trio ("Once a King There Chanced to Be"), in the Gothic Room of the Baron's Castle, where the sisters complain about their strenuous work, and mock Cinderella when she says she could dance for twenty-four hours without tiring. During the song, one can't help feeling an unusual regard for Clorinda. By the time The Faery Queen enters to join in the song, one is convinced that Miss Dare as Clorinda, who is far from ugly, may have made a far superior Cinderella.

A magnificent scene occurs in the palace as the Faery Queen appears and transforms Cinderella into Sweet Angelina: "Thou hast been humble in adversity. Be modest in thy greatness". A final chorus sings of sorrow's clouds passing. Thus the play ends with an impressive tableau. Lacy's adaptation of Rossini's music was enthusiastically accepted by the first-night audience.

G.W.H

'Who's Zenna Dare?' I jump. I've been so absorbed in reading the screen I didn't even see Kate come in. She's got the printout of Zenna Dare's picture in her hand. 'She looks pretty.'

'Just someone I'm doing a History assignment on.'

'What did she do?'

Without thinking I answer, 'She was a singer.' I think, I add to myself. That's if Miss Dare on the playbill is the same as this Zenna Dare in the picture.

'A singer?'

Then I wonder how on earth will I turn Zenna Dare into a South Australian History project? This is when I dare to think of combining the two women, Zenna Dare and Gweniver. Gweniver came out here, we know. Zenna I don't know about yet. There's still that faint hope slowly uncurling within me that I don't want to put a name to yet. It's just too far-fetched.

Kate's watching the screen now. 'She was Cinderella?'

'No. The ugly sister.'

'Oh.' The disappointment in her tone almost makes me laugh as she studies the printout. 'She doesn't look very ugly. She looks like the lady in the frame in your dr— room.' She stops herself in time. The little monkey; so she has been snooping. She carries on, obviously hoping I haven't noticed. 'Our great-grandmother.' There's an emphasis on the 'our' that I don't miss and I quickly save the part about Cinderella into Word and turn off the computer. When I skid across into my room, Kate close on my heels, the box is out of sight, the bookcase shut. I heave a sigh of relief. Steffi must have put it away. But on the bed is the letter case. A traveller's writing compendium, Steffi had called it. Kate sees it the same time as me.

'What's that?' she says, as I scoop it up.

'Just something of mine.' I'm not ready for Kate yet.

'I've never seen it before.' Accusing, as though she knows everything in my cupboard. The thought chills me; it's not impossible.

'I've got a lot of things you haven't seen before, Kate. Just forget about it.' The look on her face makes me feel as though I'm keeping her from the food she needs to survive. She's halfway up the stairs before I can say anything to placate her.

'Mu-um! Jenfa's got a secret. It's not fair.' At least Steffi knows now and will be able to distract her. I turn the letter case over. Steffi's glued the piece that was hanging; screwed in the loose brass screw. I smile. Steffi's good at this sort of thing. I put it back in the wooden box with the same amount of care I'd use on a box of Haigh's chocolates. In a way that's just what it is like — I want the papers to last, yet I get this compulsion and I have to unravel another.

GWENIVER

CORNWALL, 1845

I met a lady in the meads,
  Full beautiful — a faery's child,
Her hair was long, her foot was light,
  And her eyes were wild.

'La Belle Dame sans Merci',
John Keats 1795–1821

The boarding house in Penzance was a passable establishment. It was run by a Mrs. Hancock, who did the job with as much fervour as a captain would on his ship. She even employed bells for meal and retiring times. Nine young ladies lived there and some had places in the village. Lottie worked in Trevelyan House in the next street. Lord Trevelyan held music evenings in one of his rooms on a Sunday. It was one of the first places Mr. Drew took me to sing. All the girls in the boarding house had their own money, however small an amount. I had a whole pound Grandmama had left me, but other than that I was beholden to Mr. Drew. My lodgings were paid for by my scholarship and I did not understand at the time who was the benefactor. I was known and introduced only as the student of Mr. Drew. He had others too and some who had been so successful as to have sung at Drury Lane in London. The young Queen went to the theatre at least two or three times a week. This was my dream: to sing for the Queen. It was only a dream, of course. Even if I had won a singing competition, how could someone like me become so illustrious? Then I would remember the stories of the famous Peg, who came from a very poor family last century and became the envy of all at Covent Garden.

The singing lessons could be exciting or frightening, never tedious. The very first time, Mr. Drew had to lay his hands on either side of my diaphragm (as he called it) to show me how wrongly I was breathing, I nearly gave up altogether. No one had laid hands on me in such a way before and I could barely concentrate on his words for the embarrassment. He was not one to smile much during a lesson. He was always telling me to feel, feel the music, let it take the lead. He was quite a task-master but that made it easier, for although his dark looks could not be called handsome, his air of command and knowledge reduced me constantly to a state of awe and shivers.

On Sundays I went to the Bible Christian Chapel with Lottie, my new friend from the boarding house. I became accustomed to the exuberant 'Praise the Lords' and 'Amens' that punctuated the lively sermons. Apart from wearing black dresses, it was not unlike our Wesleyan meetings at home. On Saturdays, Mr. Drew and some other musical friends of his party would take a ride in a carriage. I became a steady member of this group and became privy to places and events I would not have known had I stayed in Camborne. If the tastes of this party conflicted with those of my parents or Lottie's chapel group I managed to suppress any misgivings at the time. I explained to myself that this was my musical education.

St. Michael's Mount was one of these places. For some reason due to his musical talents, I suppose (for he was a clever violin and pianoforte player as well as a singer, I found out later), Mr. Drew was invited to the castle by the St. Aubyns. We'd arrived at Marazion to walk across the cobbled causeway but the tide was in so Mr. Drew arranged for a boat. I will never forget the air of mystery that place birthed in me; the turrets rising out of the rock as it were, the water surrounding it making it seem I had stepped back into the very myths that explain its existence.

The great Sir John had been dead seven years so it was James who received us at the wharf. He showed us into the blue drawing room. At first I was speechless at the beautiful furniture from times long gone, and then I was invited to sing.

Afterwards, Lady St. Aubyn was beside herself. 'Don't you think she's ready, Richard? She is delightful. Oh, where did you discover her?' I tried not to mind being talked of as though I were a piece of pretty china picked up from the dirt. Richard Drew's sardonic reply shocked me at the time, 'In our county's deepest mining pit, my dear.'

'Oh, you must take her to the Assembly Rooms at Truro. Even London.' Mr. Drew was considering me as the lady spoke, with her hands clasped in delight, and I was shaken to see it was not a new thought to him. He had known all along, since he heard me in the field, what he had wanted to do with me. I cannot deny I was somewhat excited along with that nagging tug on my insides that I still encountered in his company. The man could stir in me some feeling that I could not identify. It was not the happy lurch one feels when a loved one is standing close. No, it bordered more upon fear. But fear of what? That was what puzzled me.

Outside, we took cordials and sandwiches in the western gardens, looking out to sea. Tom Ashton, a jovial young man, who sang well but wanted to be an actor, was telling us the story of the Mount. 'St. Michael appeared to fishermen in the fifth century. Can you just imagine it?' And suddenly Tom jumped up, swung himself over the stone wall and stood on the parapet.

'Careful!' We all admonished him, but it did not deter him.

'They saw him standing right over there on that ledge of rock high above the sea, in the mist. Pilgrimages were made here in the Middle Ages and there were miracles. A woman named Christina had her sight restored.' Tom landed back on the grass. 'And when the Spanish Armada came, it was the people here who saw it first and raised the alarm … with fires. Right from up there —'

Suddenly, I felt Mr. Drew's presence behind me. It was always like that; I always knew when he was in the room even when my back was turned. How could the young girl I was, who still had to watch her aitches, and with the dreams I dreamt, stand against the personal power he exerted? Especially when he held the promise of everything I yearned for?

'Come walk with me awhile, Miss Rundle,' was all he said and immediately I arose, apologising, leaving good-natured Tom in mid-sentence. Mr. Drew and I stood by the rocks looking over towards Penzance where Tom's Spanish ships must have come to conquer. 'My dear, you are becoming quite confident. The experience you have had singing in the local taverns and song and supper rooms has been quite beneficial. Yes, quite. Next week we shall visit Truro where you will sing in the Assembly Rooms, then, perhaps—'

I forgot myself enough to interrupt. 'You think I'm ready, Mr. Drew?'

'Indeed,' was all he said. He sounded amused, though he did not smile, as if there was something I did not know; but how could I imagine what my singing was like to those who listened? No one in Camborne said it was remarkable except perhaps Grandmama, and who believes their grandmothers? This was the first true encouragement that my teacher had given me this long year.

'You mean —?' I still was not sure.

'Yes, we shall go on tour, my dear.' He smiled then. 'The lessons will continue, but we shall present you in the county's best music halls —'

'And then?' Was this what I wanted? This was a point of decision —return home and marry? Or sing?

'Then, we shall see.'

It's possible he could tell by my reticence that I would need to think about it. He did not say any more, just took my arm and walked me back across the green to the others.

JENEFER

Caleb's actually asked me out for a proper date. Apparently the football clubrooms at Dutton Park have a dinner dance every Friday night. He's here early, bearing a gift. Not roses for me or chocolates, but a spare rabbit hutch from school for Hamilton to borrow. Actually it's the sweetest thing to do and it does more for me than a dozen roses would have. (Well, almost.) Kate's pouting again while Caleb explains to Hamilton.

'This can be his outside run, mate. See here?' And I watch Hamilton's gingery head bobbing next to Caleb's dark one. 'We'll put it here on the lawn and he can eat fresh grass when he feels like it.' There's hay already in the box where it's closed in and there's chicken wire on the bottom. 'Wanna go get him? See if he likes it?'

Sher Khan is very happy. Having grass sprout up through the floor of your house must be rabbit heaven. 'Is he okay now, mate?'

Hamilton smiles. 'The pineapple worked. And the hay.'

'I've been asking a guy out at the farm. He knows more than a vet even. He reckons Sher Khan shouldn't get too many hairballs now.' Hamilton gazes up at Caleb like a worshipper at a shrine. Caleb just roughs up his hair a bit while Kate stands there brooding.

The clubrooms look like any other venue in the city, like a hotel room or nightclub but without the dry ice and strobes. It's not line dancing as I feared, but a reasonable local band is playing songs from the top singles plus a few of their own. They're not bad. The dinner dance isn't restricted to teenagers either — it's nothing like a school formal. Some older people are there, ones who are interested in sport and in supporting it, I guess. One guy stops by our table and starts talking to Caleb.

'Ready for the footy, mate?'

Caleb grins. 'Sure thing, Mr Wilson. You umpiring again?'

'Do horses eat hay, mate?' And they both laugh. Mr Wilson passes on after a quick, polite nod at me.

'The football season ready to start, is it?' I ask.

'Nah, not yet. But Willy likes to be sure of his players ahead of time.'

Just then Erin and Tim come and sit at our table for a while. Tim's watching the band and makes a comment about the Celtic Festival coming up soon in the town. They must be really into it for Caleb says this band won't be playing. I wonder how he knows.

'Nice to see you out, Jenefer,' Erin says. She makes it sound like I've been cooped up in a castle for years and have just been freed, but I get the impression being seen in the clubrooms is a good move. Though if she felt like that why didn't she ask me to something? I catch her glancing from Caleb to me and I can't read her expression. I wish it wasn't so important to do what meets with everyone's approval. If I like Caleb, isn't that all that should matter? I sure hope it's enough but I don't see anyone else with someone who looks different from themselves. We are the only ones. I wonder if Caleb has noticed or if he ever thinks about it.

'C'mon, Jen-e-fer.' Caleb's pulling me up and we follow Erin and Tim onto the dance floor. He says 'Jenefer' like it's come from a song and I try to forget that everyone seems to be staring at us. Maybe I'm imagining it or they know I'm new to town, and I hope like hell it's got nothing to do with Caleb. I doubt I'd make a very good Juliet. We're dancing as a foursome, not a couple. There's more room than in places in the city, room to get entirely breathless. Then suddenly Caleb comes closer, takes my hand and swirls me round just for fun. We start laughing and just on the next turn I see a Nunga girl with her boyfriend. What chills me is the look of dislike on her face. The image of her lip curled up at me stays with me for quite a while even when I can't see her anymore. I don't dare say anything to Caleb. He might think I've imagined it, nor do I want to cause trouble.

The time goes fast, too fast; I find I'm really enjoying Caleb. He's got a look in his eyes that shows he's having fun too and that it might be to do with me. He's so funny at times, cracking stupid jokes. Ben Walker would never have been like this; he was too intent on being cool and moody to relax enough. When Caleb suggests it's time to call it a day, I agree, wondering what will come next.

It's after we get home that it all happens, not remotely what I had in mind either. It's not so late for us; I'm about to ask Caleb in for coffee as he turns off the engine, and I hear it straight away. Low sobbing. Hamilton. Caleb's out of the ute and over like a shot, kneeling beside him. Hamilton has the torch and he's jerking it around, shining it in all the flower beds, under the bushes.

'Mate. What is it?' Caleb doesn't waste time on why Hamilton isn't in bed. Hamilton dissolves into Caleb's shirt. 'I — I came out to bring Sher Khan in and s-someone turned the hutch on its side and Sher Khan — got out.' He shudders.

I think of dogs first. 'Maybe Sher Khan has gone back to the other rabbits in the bush, Hamilton. What say you come to bed and look in the morning.' I'm not used to Hamilton defying me but he does.

'No.' Quite definite. 'He'll be waiting for me to f-find him. He might be s-scared. I can't leave him out here. Not all night.' I'm hoping Caleb can think of something to get Hamilton in, but even he surprises me.

'You're right, mate. He'd want you to find him.'

'Caleb —' And I almost whisper, *What if he's not here, or worse, what if he's dead? Do we want Hamilton to find him mauled and bloody?* But Caleb moves on, helping Hamilton look. Guess he doesn't think it was dogs, then. I can't just stand around doing nothing, so I help too, but I feel useless without a torch. Hamilton's calling Sher Khan.

Will a rabbit come like a dog? By this time I'm getting wild. If not dogs, who else would do such a thing? Take a kid's pet, or let it loose?

Don't know how Caleb does it, but suddenly he's calling Hamilton over to him, softly. He's crouching down by the pepper tree. 'Mate … look here.' Then there's Hamilton's little cry, and a shaking Sher Khan is whisked inside. To Hamilton's bed, I bet.

It's too late now for coffee — we'd disturb Steffi but Caleb doesn't mind. He's tipping the hutch up the right way, puts it nearer the house. Then he comes back to me. I'm wondering what to say. Thanks for saving Hamilton's mind? How do you say thanks for that? Caleb doesn't say anything either. The yellow light from the street lamp shines through the pepper tree. I remember that bit, just as Caleb lifts a hand and runs his finger down my cheek. It makes me lift my chin so it doesn't stop and that's when he kisses me.

'Thanks,' I finally say, before he swings himself into the ute, but we both know what it's really for.

GWENIVER

CORNWALL, JUNE 1846

For neither men nor angel can discern
Hypocrisie, the onely evil that walks
Invisible, except to God alone ...

Paradise Lost, John Milton 1608–74

Midsummer's Eve in Penzance: what gaiety there was. We all, Tom Ashton, Lily and Mr. Drew's other students, enjoyed the madness in the town that night. Young men with burning banners ran through the streets; bonfires lit up otherwise murky street corners; people burnt candles on their doorsteps. All the young boys and girls began dancing, forming long lines, the last two making an archway for the others to run through.

The next day was Midsummer's Day and the place was thronged with people. There were cattle, donkeys and horses for sale. In the market square, amidst the noise of a brass band, standings were erected for the sale of fruit and sweets. The ice-cream cart was a great attraction. I had never seen one before, nor had the children who lived there, by the way they crowded around it. Mr. Drew, I, and the others strolled through it all: the booths for small shows; the peep shows (not that we ladies looked); freaks of nature; a deplorable cock fight on the green. There was even a small circus. Tom enjoyed himself in the shooting gallery and even threatened to join the boxing booth. It was about this time, as we were making way for a horse and cart to move through the crowd, that a serious argument occurred between two parties.

Crackers were discharged which so enraged one group that serious consequences would have ensued had a spirited gentleman on horseback not dispersed the crowd. It was after this incident that Mr. Drew hired a carriage, as if he had had his fill of Midsummer's Day in Penzance.

'Come, I have something to show you,' he said to me. The others were not invited to accompany us.

He drove the vehicle himself and we followed the coast all the way to a pretty place called Cove of Lamorna. At the time I did not think of the song I sang at the fair in Camborne. It may be that he remembered. Perhaps that was why he took me so far.

The sea was up high by then, being late afternoon, splashing onto the rocks, yet the cove was sheltered. He led me down there, taking my hand wherever the path was rough, as I manoeuvred my full skirt and numerous petticoats that he insisted I wear.

'Gweniver.' I did not start at the use of my first name. Being my teacher he had early dispensed with calling me Miss Rundle when we were alone. I was staring out to sea, wondering how well I would choose my path. Nor was I altogether thinking of the way across the rocks.

'Gweniver, see that rock out in the water?' I fixed my gaze where he was pointing, noted the spindrift rising round the blackness of the lone rock. It put me in mind of the wrecker stories Clarice would tell us at night years ago.

'There is said to be a lady who sits there, showing herself before a storm. She sits and sings most plaintively if there is to be a wreck, and all along the shore, the spirits have echoed her in low moaning voices.' I shivered as he paused.

'Young men have swum off to the rock, lured by her songs, but they never return. I am not so young and mindless, but Gweniver,' and here he turned me towards him. 'You are that woman to me. I have swum to your rock and I can never return. You lured me from the very first day I heard you singing in that field.

'Come with me, Gweniver. You have the talent to take even London by storm, let alone Cornwall.'

'But —'

'No buts.'

He was smiling, sure of what I would answer, but how could I explain? Sing, I must. I knew that much and so did he, but what was involved in the proposition he was offering? Even then I did not know, could not know, he would want my very soul. There was still a look in his eyes that disturbed me at times, even then, when he was finally singing my praises and smiling. As for luring him, could I believe him? What was he saying? He took my hand, turned it over and kissed the palm but I wanted to snatch it away. It felt cold, unprotected, and he kissed it again. Naturally,

I thought he must know the kind of family I came from: simple, strict, Wesleyan. Surely he understands. And so I relaxed. My skin warmed and his dark eyes looked up from my palm.

'I care for you, Gweniver,' he whispered. Did I hear him truly? Was it loud enough for me to hear above the noise on the rocks? Or was it my fancy that made me relax, made me think that he would not hurt me, that he would want the best for me. For that is how I understood love, and so I made my decision: I went on tour.

But he lied, for I was the one who was lured, not he.

JENEFER

Gweniver is unfolding before my eyes. How difficult it must have been after being part of all that cultural scene in Cornwall — the music, a castle on a mountain in the sea — and all of a sudden she lands in Woop Woop. Man, do I know how that feels! Yet she must have got used to it somehow. She married Redvers, had piles of kids. But something doesn't ring true. How does she get to marry Redvers if she's so set on not marrying, and why couldn't she anyway? When I'm in my room like this, sitting in the window, I can almost see her shadow here. Feel her sadness, her longing for something that I don't understand.

Zenna Dare is even more elusive — she's my enigmatic unsung tune — and it's because of her that Caleb and I take a trip to the city. It's the first time I've been since we moved to Kapunda. Caleb comes round the back to pick me up. Because it's Saturday, the kids are there, still eating Weet-Bix and bananas. Hamilton smiles up at him through the bleary puffiness of his face. Steffi's watching him closely. Wonder if he's told her about Sher Khan getting out last night. Kate looks baleful — it's the only word for it. Not just the woeful meaning either. The calculated malice in her expression at times can be alarming. Guess she wants to come with us, but you can't have your little sister with you all the time. I soon forget about it as we walk out to the gate.

'The sheik said I could have the ute today.'

'The sheik?' Whoever he is, he's generous with his ute; maybe it's a spare.

Caleb grins. 'That's what everyone calls the guy who owns the camel farm. Even wears the baggy Afghan clothes that the original cameleers used to wear.'

'This I have to see,' I murmur. But not today. I look up at Caleb. He's teasing, 'Next week?' he says and I know it's another date. I'm going to have to learn to drive. Dad always said we'd wait until we got to Kapunda. 'It'll be easier in the country,' he said.

We drive to the Gawler railway station and catch the train. At the beginning of the year I said Kapunda was hicksville — driving to Gawler to get the train! Water-bag trip! — and I almost feel traitorous when I remember my thoughts on the way up in January. Now I love having the extra time to watch Caleb as he talks; his hands on the wheel as they rise and fall. They talk too. Especially when he sings along to the radio.

The State Library's not far up North Terrace but I couldn't care how far anything is anymore. When we pass the museum, Caleb tells me his mum goes there a lot.

'Why the museum?' And I wonder how far I can joke about his family — 60,000 years of genealogy held in the museum?

'They've got a good records section where Nungas can come and work out who their mobs were.'

I think of the excitement I feel, just knowing I'll find out a bit more today. 'How much has your mum found?'

'That we're of the Ngadjuri mob. We are the *walpa juri*, the peppermint gum people. They lived near the Light River, even further up and way out east too, before the Goonyas came.' He glances at me as he says this and I think about *before the Goonyas came*. So much still that I'm not sure of and I don't realise it until moments like these. Then he grins. One of his grins can dispel any tension. 'Unfortunately, only the bad eggs got their name in print, so it's hard to trace anyone.'

In the library I find the same thing. Even though Zenna Dare may have been a public figure she's extremely difficult to find. There's nothing at all in the online catalogue. Even when I plug in 'Nineteenth century theatre in Cornwall' there's nothing. I score with 'British Theatre' though and write down the Dewey numbers. Caleb's brought a book to read in case he gets bored. I grin as my eyes scale the stacks of books — looks like millions and he brings another one? He reckons there won't be any fantasy novels in here and I can see his point. I leave him in a comfy chair while I start searching. Blue stacks, red stacks and even more in storage. I find the shelf of British Theatre and check the indexes of all the most interesting ones but no Zenna Dare. Tons of stuff on theatres in Drury Lane and Covent Garden. Nothing that I think I need.

Steffi would tell me at this point to think laterally. And I try. If Zenna Dare was in *Cinderella*, does that make her a singer? *Opera*. Of course. Back to the catalogue and I take down numbers for English opera. Nothing for Cornwall, as usual. Isn't anybody writing about Cornwall? I walk past

Caleb on the way back to the stacks — he's furtively eating a KitKat and grins. He points to his watch; he's getting hungry. He promised me lunch but I stay strong, smile and keep walking.

At the 790s there are hundreds of books on music. I find some opera ones; pull out one called 'British Opera'. But there is no Zenna Dare in the index. With a sinking feeling I realise they're not going to give space to someone who sang as the ugly sister in Cinderella. I'm expecting too much. Then I see this old book. There's no dust cover, just pale green cloth. It reminds me of the books in the Gawler library. I blow on it before I look inside: 1950. No one's read it since then either, by the look of it. It's called *Great Singers of English Opera*. Mostly it's all about people who spent their whole lives on the stage, and there's no index! I groan. I can't stand books with no indexes, and before I knew about Zenna Dare I couldn't have cared less.

I flip through the chapters, trying to get the date right — mid nineteenth century — and all of a sudden I see it. The 'Z' is hard to miss. She's mentioned as a member of the cast of an opera in the Theatre Royal, Drury Lane, London, in November 1846. *The Bohemian Girl*. That's all it says. I keep it open to copy. My knowledge of opera is zilch. Who was the Bohemian girl? I'm glancing over the whole shelf of books now — this is too big — like looking for the back of an earring on the beach. I see a book called *The Stories of Opera* and I look up *The Bohemian Girl* in the contents. It's there: the whole story about how this girl called Arline is kidnapped as a child and brought up as a gypsy and she falls in love with a gypsy guy. But apparently it wasn't cool to fall in love with gypsies in those days. Nothing much changes, eh? It all turns out okay in the end. The guy is really a prince and she can marry him after all. I've typed some notes on my iPad and am just about to take the books to the photocopier when Caleb finds me.

'I've finished my book,' he says in a loud stage whisper. 'I'll go and check out a music shop. I shall return.' He's funny and I nod happily at him. It's my cue to offer to come but I don't. He blows me a kiss as he turns to look back at me and I almost forget what I was going to do next. Almost.

It's when I'm waiting in line for the photocopier, reading the bit about Zenna Dare being in the opera, that I see this sentence: *Reviews of the day raved over the opening performance; how the debut appearance of Mr. Drew's new student, Miss Dare, charmed the audience.*

Reviews! Newspapers. This was London. Was there such a thing as a *London Times*? After an age in the copy line, I go to the reference desk and ask. An unsmiling librarian gives me access to a computer and I find out for myself. It takes a while. I end up with the history of the Tower of London and all sorts of rubbish I don't need to know until I finally hit on a site that gives the names of the London newspapers through the ages. I find one that fits the dates: *London Times*, and a magazine called *Illustrated London News*. Bingo! I head towards the newspaper section. I'm so glad Caleb's happy in a music shop somewhere — this will take forever.

The library assistant has to show me how to use the microfiche viewer for the *London Times* and I wonder why this hasn't been put online. I scroll down the index. Nothing. *The Illustrated London News* is in the magazine section. Crossing my fingers, I start sliding down mountains of columns. In those days they didn't put articles where you think they would be — like it doesn't help to look up at the back or in an arts section. At least I know which month and year to look in. I'm up to the 27th of November before I find it. And I print it out. This time I'm sure it's Zenna. Her first name is even mentioned.

There's just one more thing I have to do. Caleb hasn't come back yet so I go into Mortlock Library, the part of the State Library that stores local material. This place is even more awesome than the old library buildings at Gawler and Kapunda. This is huge, ancient dark wood, and floors within floors of books like never-ending reflecting mirrors. I stand still, watching a librarian climb dark brown stairs with carved rails, a stack of papers in her arms, and I suddenly realise something: this is what I want to do. Puzzles. Piecing together people's lives. I've never known before. Whenever old aunts at family dinners would ask what I'm going to be when I grow up (pul-lease), I would always be so embarrassed. I never knew what to say.

I ask at the desk how to check arrivals into South Australia and get shown this archaic card system and the famous green books. Shipping and passenger lists are pointed out to me and I hope Caleb doesn't come back too soon. There's no Zenna Dare on the little cards and without that info I can't look up the shipping or passenger lists. I find Gweniver's arrival on the cards under 'Rundle' though; the Tremaynes too. I find the corresponding passenger list and there in faded light ink in even messier writing than Gweniver's is Redvers' name: *Redvers Tremayne, 15 yrs.* A Harry Tremayne too, five years. There's a scrawl next to his name and I just make it out: *died at sea.* I stand there transfixed, staring at this huge page that some ship's purser had written on, over one and a half centuries ago. *Died at sea.* I can feel the sting behind my eyes and the page blurs slightly. Why should this affect me? I never knew them. Yet I know what Caleb would say.

I shut the book and try Gweniver's passenger list. She's there. But I can't find Zenna Dare anywhere. She didn't come with Gweniver or never came at all. Maybe my elusive tune can start playing in earnest at last. I approach the desk from the side and bravely ask about it.

'As far as can be known then, no one of the name of Zenna Dare has entered the state. The cards even show if someone came from interstate,' the librarian says. It feels as if she's looking down her nose at me. I wonder if librarians ever feel like breaking out of that disciplined reserve and saying Duh.

'She never came?' It must be my tone of voice for the librarian sounds a little kinder. 'Are you sure it's her real name?'

I have to close my eyes a second, hope stirring like a laser probing my mind. 'What do you mean?'

'Maybe she married just before she came?'

I calm down again. Haven't thought of that one. 'I don't know. How can I check?'

I'm told about the *International Genealogical Index*. 'It's on the web.' And I start checking marriages. There is no Zenna Dare, either married or born. Armed with this information I approach the desk for further orders.

'Not all parishes are listed, of course. It's possible she slipped through. Some records were burnt in fires.'

I think I must be tired. This is not as much fun when you keep drawing blanks. According to Mortlock Library, Zenna Dare never existed, yet she's on a playbill in the box (well, Miss Dare is). She's been an ugly sister, and she sang in *The Bohemian Girl*. I have the review to prove it.

I sit down, defeated, in the foyer and wait for Caleb. *Was it her real name?* Those words keep ricocheting into my head. And I let myself listen to the opening bars of Zenna's tune at last: my alternative theory. When you think about it, the name doesn't sound real. What sort of name is *Zenna* for an Cornish girl in the 1840s? But I need more clues to be sure. I get out the review and read it through.

ILLUSTRATED LONDON NEWS

THE BOHEMIAN GIRL

Drury Lane

Nov. 27th 1846

"The Bohemian Girl" opened at Drury Lane last night and if the delight of the audience can be used as an indication, the opera should have a successful season. It has marked the debut of a Miss Zenna Dare, the new protegée of Mr. Richard Drew. The question on everyone's lips is: where has Mr. Drew found this songbird? She does not act badly and there are possibly better singers but Miss Dare's charm consists in making one forget them all. What she offers is so completely hers, so harmoniously fresh and lovable that one allows oneself to be captured and to embrace it with pleasure.

Mr. Richard Drew consented to take part in the performance as the gypsy lover and also played the violin with great intricacy of fingering. The company gasped at the dexterity he showed playing Balfe's haunting gypsy tunes and the sweetness of tone rendered his performance a treat of the most superior kind.

Miss Dare's sweet and mellow voice blended with Mr. Drew's baritone, making one's imagination fly right into the drama. The sense of intimacy between the two singers in the forest glade almost made one feel an intruder on a private love scene.

L.K.H

Richard Drew! Gweniver has written of a Mr Drew. Lady St Aubyn called him Richard. He must be the same. Is this proof? Dare I think it at last: was Gweniver actually Zenna Dare? A stage name? Was she that good? Her journal just sounded like she was having singing lessons and then singing in taverns and special song and supper rooms in Cornwall. But London? It could fit; she did say Mr Drew was thinking of it and it was her dream. Maybe she managed to achieve it after all. Though, in the Cinderella piece I printed off the web, there was another student of Mr Drew's, a Miss Ginny Rivers. G.R. for Gweniver Rundle — wouldn't that be more likely?

And maybe Zenna Dare was her friend — after all, they sang together. If so, who was Zenna Dare?

I don't get a chance to dwell on it just then for Caleb suddenly appears.

'Lunch?' I don't know how he can still be in a good mood after I've made him wait so long. It's almost three. Caleb takes me across the road to the Blue Lemon. I want to pay but he tells me he has more money than I do at the moment. That's probably true, so I just remember it'll be my turn next time. I choose a chicken, avocado and cream cheese baguette. He has a hot BBQ one. We eat them out in the street at a table with a red-striped umbrella that reminds me of a postcard I've seen of Paris.

Just then I get the proverbial shock of my life. 'Hi, Jenefer!' It's Amy, Sokha, Ben Walker (would you believe), and another guy I don't know. I see Amy's glance take all of Caleb in. 'We've just been to the movies,' and they tell us what it was about. I suggest that they join us but it's Ben who says they have to keep moving. He's got a weird look on his face; I'm surprised he doesn't hide what he's thinking more carefully — I can hear it loud and clear and no doubt Caleb can too. *This is who you get to go out with in the sticks? You poor girl and you could have had me, if you'd stayed.* Even Sokha has little to say when I introduce Caleb. Guess she's remembering how we talked about the drunks at Victoria Square and look at me now. I can tell what Amy's thinking too for she looks back at Ben after she glances at Caleb — like what sort of comparison is there? Blond, cool Ben and an 'Abo' from the back of beyond? It unnerves me and for two reasons: one, that I would have liked them to be happy for me, and two, that's just what I would have thought a few months ago too.

After they move on, Caleb and I just sit quietly eating for a while. My baguette doesn't taste half as good as it did before. Finally Caleb says, 'They your friends, eh?'

I don't say anything for the confusion has set in. I know I don't fit into Kapunda yet, although I have fun with Caleb, but now I don't fit with my old friends either. Have I changed that much in a few months? And why couldn't they see that if I liked Caleb he must be okay? Why did they see that he was a Nunga first? And look at him as though his skin being darker means it's thicker too? It's Caleb who tries to put me at ease when it's me who should be apologising to him. 'Don't worry about it.' He sounds weary, like he's used to ignorant reactions.

'Jenefer,' and he reaches over and touches my hand, 'tell me what you found in the library.'

I make an effort. After all, that's what he's trying to do. Can I do any less? And I tell him my secret deepest hope. 'Um — I think that Zenna Dare is real. But her name might not be.'

He gives a short laugh. 'How's that?'

'I think it's a stage name. You know, when ladies were in the theatre years ago they had a professional name. More respectable, maybe?' I gathered from what I read today that singing was an okay profession but acting was still considered suspect. 'Zenna was a singer, I reckon.' Maybe it's the look on my face but he catches onto what I'm thinking; what has been lurking at the bottom of my brain ever since I saw the two photos of Gweniver and Zenna Dare.

'So you think your grandmother was a singer?' He's left off the 'greats' as though Gweniver is alive now, and I can see the incredulity on his face. 'Don't you think you would have heard about it?'

That does make me stop chewing. It's true, a family would surely have been proud of something like that, and passed it on.

'What about the papers she's written? Does she mention Zenna Dare?'

My hope is sinking fast again. 'Not so far — not in the ones I've managed to work out.'

Caleb's gazing at me; there are lines between his eyes. I think he doesn't understand so I explain. 'I'm typing them up, so I've got stage one ready to show Ms East. Otherwise it's double handling.'

'There must be some you haven't read yet.' I can tell by his tone that he thinks I'm crazy. I guess he would have read them all at once. But they're not that easy to read. Just deciphering one takes ages. 'I'll get to them. Then I'll put them all in order. With some background stuff thrown in they'll make an excellent independent study.'

Caleb's just finished his baguette; leans back, wiping his hands. He's not looking at me as he says this next bit. 'And what will your Aunt Dorie think of that?'

I decide not to answer him. Aunt Dorie's in the Dark Ages and I don't agree with her attitude, but Caleb's tone makes me think. Like at what point will Zenna Dare become familial, someone personal, rather than a mystery I enjoy researching? The look on Caleb's face matches his tone and it annoys me. Meeting my old friends has put a sharp edge to a mood I've never shown Caleb before. This is my family, not his. What right has he got to question my motives? He's right about being able to tell what people are feeling, though. I never thought about it much before, but I reckon I know what's in his head right now, as if it were in bold print, and nor do I appreciate it. I don't like feeling that he's disappointed in me.

We walk down North Terrace to the train. It hurts how we don't look like a couple; we're both somewhere else, yet we sit in the same seat. By the time the train lurches to a start I'm trying to think of a way to get our old closeness back but Caleb beats me to it. He leans over and whispers, 'Sorry.' Amazing what that one little word does. I smile back. 'Me too.'

'No. It's me. I've been brought up to think family stuff is too important to muck around with but I shouldn't have dumped that on you. You might think differently about it.' Caleb's really trying. It's hard to imagine what someone else may understand or believe; what memories they may have that affect their waking hours. When have I ever tried that? And I slip my arm through his. Move a little closer. He grins down at me — his usual easy-going grin. It's just at that point I look up and surprise a look of unveiled disgust on an old woman's face. I feel like saying, 'What?' I must have made some sound for Caleb glances over too, but that's all it is, a glance, and he's looking at me again.

The woman doesn't stop staring at me. 'What's her problem?' I'm hissing, and I nearly ask her what she's looking at. 'Ignore her. It's me, not you.' This from Caleb. *Caleb*?

'You're kidding.' I can't believe it — twice in one day.

'Yeah, nice white girl going out with a black fella.' It's incredible hearing him talk like this, as though he's a Nunga from the interior who never gets to see the city. Is he joking? The crooked twist to his mouth says it all though — in that woman's eyes I must be a slut.

'I've never been looked at like that. It's obscene.'

'Better get used to it.' I can hear the rest of the words in his head, *if you keep going places with me*. No one usually looks at *me*, Jenefer Tremayne. That's it, I'm invisible. I always have been. Not today. Everyone sees Caleb. I check out their faces. Most try not to notice but the people closest have varying expressions ranging from curiosity to pity to open appraisal on a young guy's face as he stares at me. It's disgusting. I feel dirty all of a sudden and it has nothing to do with Caleb.

I turn back to him. 'But you're not scruffy or drunk, or causing a scene.' I feel like saying he's a babe, but now mightn't be the right time.

'Bet they've seen someone who was, though.'

'That's not you.'

'Tell them that.' I feel the first touch of bitterness in Caleb's tone and it saddens me. Would he feel this bitterness all the time if he was looked at like this every day? Surely not Caleb, who puts kids at ease, so sure of himself, he can joke at school about being Indigenous. But not here. Here, there's no joke.

'How can they tell anyway?' He almost glares at me then and I realise it wasn't what I meant. I could kick myself; I should have said something supportive like, 'What's it to them?'

Suddenly the man across the aisle from me leans over. 'Is he bothering you?' I'm so astounded I can't say anything. *Bothering me? Caleb? Creative, peace-making Caleb who looks for a little rabbit in the dark so a kid can be happy? Caleb, who can understand what's in my head? It's that guy over there, thinking kinky stuff about me, who's bothering me.*

'Of course not,' I manage to say. 'He's my … friend.' I was about to say boyfriend and Caleb knows it. He has a different look in his eyes now and it's just for me. Nothing has been said about our friendship — it didn't need to be. I like being with him and he must feel the same or he wouldn't keep dropping me home after school or coming with me on these treasure hunts. Nor would he have kissed me under the pepper tree last night. His eyebrows are raised in a question and I say, 'I like being your friend.' I whisper 'friend' as though it's a different word, and his eyes go a darker brown. The laughing lines on either side of his mouth start to twitch and in that moment something small and hard melts inside me and I couldn't care less what everyone thinks. I lean over and kiss him.

GWENIVER

CORNWALL, 1846

Here lie deposited
The mortal remains of
Mr Joseph Antonia Emidy
who departed this life
on the 23rd of April,
1835

Devoted to thy soul inspiring strains
Sweet Music! thee he hail'd his chief delight
And with fond zeal that shunn'd not toil nor pain
His talent soar'd and genius marked his flight.

I remember the day I saw Joseph Emidy's grave. Afterwards, Mr. Drew took me to a concert at the Assembly Rooms in Truro. I recall little of getting to the place but for numerous stairs and passageways. When it was my turn to sing, I reached the platform where I stood next to the pianoforte and a twelve-piece orchestra, no less. I looked down onto the gallery and up to the balcony surrounding three whole sides of the hall and saw hundreds, no, a thousand people. I nearly lost my nerve. All the gentlemen seemed to be smoking cigars and had a glass in front of them. But there were ladies present too, it being Thursday evening.

The members of the Harmonic Society had put together

a program and I was asked to sing two songs, then there was an encore. Before Mr. Drew could rescue me I was begged to sing another. I could feel the music crash like a powerful drum inside of me. My singing was a mere response to the vibration that resonated within, possessing and shaking me all the way to my heart. I couldn't have fought it even if I had a mind to. Truly I thought I would burst with all that sound inside and I knew that this was what I was born to do.

Mr Emidy had often played the violin there, music he had composed himself. He used to be a slave and I found that astonishing. A captain of a ship saw him in a Lisbon orchestra leading the violins and took him aboard ship and would not let him go. Years later, he was given his freedom and set ashore in Falmouth, where he lived and taught.

It would have been wonderful to have met him. Singing in a place where I knew he had been made me feel such an affinity with him. I was no less a slave than he was: a caged bird, yet I was working out a dream as no doubt so was he. What an impression his story made on me; his spirit, creativity and humility all rolled together in one soul. Even Mr. Drew had a good word to say on his behalf.

Mr. Charles Hempel was there too and said how delightfully I sang. He hoped he would hear more of me. The whole experience inspired me to keep at my musical studies even if I was a little in awe of Mr. Drew. Occasionally, he looked at me as if I were some freshly baked game he was to eat for dinner. Yet at other times he was almost amiable, telling me gossip about the music halls, taking me to places where I was to sing, so I became used to noisy audiences full of men who had eaten and drunk too much.

At that point, I still did not receive any money of my own; Mr. Drew handled everything and gave me whatever I needed. He decided what I should wear, which songs to sing. He favoured silk, muslin too. Mama always thought muslin was frivolous and it took me a while to feel at home in it. For months I felt like a rich cousin I never knew I had. Mr. Drew liked to see me in blue, never green. Green was unlucky for the stage, he said. So many petticoats, tiers of frills, and a bustle that he insisted on since it was fashionable that year. Bodices that Da would say showed far too much shoulder and neck. I never seemed to be able to train my shoulders to slope just the way they should. One dress had a neckline almost level with my armpits. I am sure even Mama would have quailed at it, though it was lovely.

It was not long after Truro that Mr. Drew employed a girl to help with my hair; all those curls on either side, to stitch a hem if need be, to lace up the corset, and make new dresses. He bought a beautiful, velvet cape for my travel in the carriage. I never knew if he did the same for the other students and I presumed it all came from the scholarship I won that day at the fair.

It was beginning to stifle me that I felt like a kept woman, but what was the alternative? How could I, a simple girl, achieve a dream like mine without a guide such as Mr. Drew? I had only heard of those places before; would never have the means to go, let alone have been invited to sing. My goodness, if I were still in Camborne I would be like Mary, being courted by someone like Will Trengove!

Fore Street
Camborne

February 1846

Dearest Gweniver,

We hope you are enjoying your singing lessons. We miss you so much and not only when the washing and baking needs to be done. James Penwith has proposed marriage to Gladys. He works in the mine with Da. Mama is not pleased but Gladys is weary of looking after the rest of us, I am thinking.

Do you remember Will? He is Annie Trengove's brother. He has taken to talking to me after chapel. He sings in the choir. He says he does not want to stay a miner here, earning three pounds a month and working eight hours a day underground in air that's so bad the candles won't burn. He wants to go to South Australia. There is land for all, apparently. What do you think of that, then? 'Tis a long way away.

Clarice has taken a teaching post and Mama would not let Tommy go down the mine with Da on account of what happened to Georgie. Tom turned twelve last week so Da apprenticed him to old Hawker, the blacksmith.

When shall we see you again? Everyone sends their wishes for your success.

Your loving sister, Mary.

JENEFER

We decide to visit the camel farm, but we go to Caleb's house on the way. Must admit I'm nervous — what if they don't like me? There isn't just his mum, like I thought. His widowed aunt and her five kids live there too. 'No point just Mum and me in a big house,' he'd said. No wonder he's good with Hamilton.

As soon as I walk in, his mum's there, smiling. She's so sweet. I can see this shy, creative person who just wants to shed goodwill. It's amazing after what she's been through. Though from everything Caleb had said about her, I didn't expect anything else. Kids walk in and out, getting drinks, smiling. It could have been a perfect visit except for Chloe, his cousin. It was when we went into the lounge. She was already there, watching the TV with her arm round a little girl Kate's age, and when she turned to see us I must have looked as if I'd seen a ghost. She was the same girl I noticed at the dinner dance — the one I caught looking at me as though she could kill me.

She's a bit younger than me, and the look on her face still says more than hurtful words could say. She makes me feel I have no right to be going out with Caleb at all. Like I was stealing someone's only lamb when I have a flock of sheep of my own. It affects me even more than the trip to town last week. I guess because Caleb's family matters more. What if she puts him off me?

I mention it on the way to the camel farm. 'It's not you personally, Jenefer. She'll get over it when she knows you as well as I do.' I wish I could say the same for my friends. At least Steffi and Dad don't mind me going places with him.

'You seemed to know what I was like straight away.' Or thought he did.

He grins. 'But I'm a guy.'

'What's that supposed to mean?'

He ducks from imaginary blows. 'Okay. I won't get into that one.' Then he sobers up. 'Seriously, Jenefer, it can be hard for some. Your mob kicked us off our land, took away what we believed in and left us with nothing.'

'But that wasn't me.' Suddenly I'm annoyed and I remember Alicia Tilbrook in History during the week. We shouldn't have to say sorry at all, she said. *I didn't do it. Did you?* And she looked so angelic as she said it too. At the time I attacked head on; her words sounded so hollow. She had no idea what 'it' was and I told her. *They only want our land*, was her next startling statement. No matter that Ms East tried to explain that certain land rules were in place. I couldn't believe Alicia would say it aloud. Whose land was it in the first place, for heaven's sake? Was there a treaty signed that passed it all over? Imagine if Caleb did History and he was there. Doubt if even that would bother

Alicia; it's like she doesn't think he has feelings. Tim calls her Ku Klux Alice. What is the answer to someone like Alicia? No one seems to know, not even the government, it seems. The truly horrifying thought is I had no idea about it either three months ago, and now Chloe looks at me the exact same way I think about Alicia Tilbrook. The way that makes you wonder if there is such a thing as being part of a community and being held responsible for what it did.

'Chloe's young yet,' Caleb says. 'She's just trying to hang onto who she is. She'll learn to let go of the anger in time.'

His mother's learnt to forgive, he said once. Is it something that you learn? Forgiving, letting go of anger? And what about him? Has he learnt? Suddenly I can't think straight. This is it, then. He really thinks all this too, doesn't he? Like Chloe. Why is he spending time with me? I'm not stupid, I know he likes me. But why? Just attraction? Deep down, will he hate me in the end?

'So what about you? You feel like that too? It's the way you were brought up.' I want to say more. I should just ask him to take me home. How could this have worked? We're too different. Even his own people think so.

Then he says no.

'No what?' I don't care I sound bitchy. This is most probably the last I'll see of him anyway.

'I wasn't brought up like Chloe. After the Salvation Army found Mum she believed all that too. She still tells the old stories through her art, goes to schools, but she doesn't have that bitterness Auntie Bet has.' He turns to me. 'Mum is a hell of a lot easier to live with than Auntie Bet. Hating immigrant Australians for what happened isn't going to solve anything.'

I can't stop myself in time. 'So you go out with one? To prove you don't hate us? You're doing your bit. Is that it?' I don't believe I'm saying this. I'm destroying something I want to keep, but it's like a fire in the bush that jump-starts nearby trees without my meaning it to. Soon everything will be burnt.

Caleb's pulled over, switches the engine off. He turns me to face him. His hand is on my arm; I can feel it shaking. He's saying 'no' but I can hardly see him for the smoke of what I'm doing. 'Jenefer. Jen.' It's starting to clear. I was just upset. Was I jealous? She lives with him. Can cousins feel for each other like I feel for Caleb? It's not until later when Caleb explains about moieties, the complex clan laws of who everyone can marry, that I understand; he couldn't have a relationship with Chloe even if he wanted to.

'It was only you, Jenefer. I wasn't thinking of anything else. I just liked you.' Why is he bothering to be so kind after what I almost did? How fragile feelings are. And I wonder how strong they can be too. 'I'm sorry.' My eyes are wet and he holds me close to him. He's warm; I can feel his heart running, chasing something that was getting away; catching up.

'I don't want to lose you, Jen. We are just two people who like each other. I never wanted it to get complicated.'

'Me neither.' I look up and then he's kissing me. It's different from before — I feel like the box when he helped me open it, caressing it, finding out its secrets before it gives them up — and I never want it to stop, never. But we'd better. An image of Steffi with a fiery crucifix in her hand as I come home pregnant flashes into my mind and won't budge. Steffi may not be my real mum but she's sure imparted all her Catholic morals. I had no idea that when the crunch came they'd actually work. Bummer. Bet I'm the last virgin in Year 12. Even Erin does it with Tim. Though she only does because he wants to. I'd rather have a guy who cares about me, not one who can't wait to do it.

'We'd better stop.' We're not sitting anymore and Caleb's suddenly still, leaning his chin down on my shoulder.

'Yeah, you're right.' His voice sounds husky and he gives this shuddering sigh and I wonder if he understands. Salvation Army, he'd said. It's possible he's been told all the same stuff.

'It's just that —' I wonder if I should say what I'm thinking or just blame the handbrake poking into my back, but he puts a finger on my mouth. 'It's cool.' And suddenly I realise what it was I liked about him that first day of school.

We think it's best to pick up Kate and Hamilton and take them out to the camel farm with us. Besides, Hamilton's been asking for ages. The farm is incredible — Shetland ponies, miniature horses, donkeys, and of course, the camels. There is this huge bull camel called Horace, sitting in the paddock near the home run.

'You can pat him,' Caleb says with a grin. I'm not sure if he's joking or not. 'Just grab hold of his nose rope and he'll do whatever you want.'

It's Hamilton who walks up to Horace. Kate and I watch, we're not all that scared — I just hope Hamilton and Caleb don't notice we're not still with them. Imagine the teasing. Horace hasn't bitten Hamilton yet, or spat, or stamped on him, so I venture closer, a little shadow half a step behind me. Fortunately I'm right there when Caleb turns around. I can't say I've ever been into camels, but Horace doesn't look bad close up. There's a little cute one, running around its mother. They all seem pleased to see Caleb.

'What do you do, when you come?' They don't look as if they'd need brushing like horses.

'Feed them, ride a few. Especially if there are races coming up. Clean out the shed. Take some out bush. When all that's done I mend fences.'

'Fences?'

He points at the camels in the paddock. 'See that big bull? That's Josh. A coupla weeks ago he charged right through the fence. My job to fix it. The sheik's getting old now. I'm his right-hand man. Might go with him up north when the races are on up there.'

I'm quiet, thinking about Caleb being away and wonder how Mr Wilson will cope with one of his players missing. Kate's trying to get a pony to come to her. It won't budge but she doesn't seem to mind — being out here where it's so wide and open puts her in a good mood. She's not annoyed there's mud on her sneakers and she's even smiling at Hamilton scratching Horace's nose. This must be when she gets the idea of joining the town pony club. Then I glance back at Caleb; he's watching Kate too. He looks fluid, as though he's been poured out onto the paddock and will grow here, bending with every breeze. Then he turns; sees me watching him and gives me one of his widest grins. I catch my breath at the beauty of it. And I know why he likes this job.

When I'm home I check my email and messages.

From: Jenefer Tremayne
To: Royal Cornish Library
Subject: Zenna Dare

Dear Librarian

I have found your site on the Cornish Web Ring and wonder if you can help me.

I'm researching nineteenth century opera or theatre in Cornwall with particular reference to a Miss Zenna Dare and/or Gweniver Rundle. Do you know of any resources that I may be able to find here in Australia?

Thank you

Jenefer Tremayne

From: Ross Shelley
To: Jenefer Tremayne
Subject: Zenna Dare

Dear Jenefer

I'm very sorry I haven't been able to get back to you sooner. My server has been down. I don't know much about Zenna Dare, except that she was a mysterious singer in the nineteenth century; mysterious because no one knew of her background and little is known even today. She sang in London for Queen Victoria, began a sensational but short career and suddenly disappeared. Her identity has been carefully guarded. Most singers and actresses were quite free with their real names and these, along with their stage aliases, can be found on the web, but not Zenna Dare's. It may have been her real name, of course.

Hope this still helps

Ross of Ross's World of Photographs.

Her real name? I hope not, for if it is my phantom tune will never be played.

GWENIVER

KAPUNDA, 1850

Little think'st thou, poore flower,
Whom I have watch'd sixe or seaven dayes,
And seene thy birth, and seene what every houre
Gave to thy growth, thee to this height to raise,
And now dost laugh and triumph on this bough,
Little think'st thou
That it will freeze anon, and that I shall
To morrow finde thee falne, or not at all.

'The Blossome',
John Donne 1572–1631

There is little opportunity to write much since our days here are very busy. All the household tasks we did in Cornwall still have to be done, with less help. Every day we rise at five and there is the dusting, shaking of rugs, sweeping, and cleaning out the fireplaces. Candles have to be made, the butter too. It takes hours. There is no yeast and Mary makes bread called damper. The outside of it looks too dirty to eat since we make it in the ashes but the inside is passable. Mary has an open fireplace in the kitchen with a Dutch oven hanging over it and she has another pot we bury in the coals to bake the pasties in. Even the garden has to be tended so we can have vegetables and herbs.

Yesterday I walked down the street to help with the shopping. Mr. Whittaker has most things in his shop, even a Posting Office set up in one corner, but Mary and I make no use of his services now. Gladys has not written to Mary since her part in helping me, though I am sure Mama would have sent us a letter if she could write. At least Kapunda is a friendly place and everyone seems most hospitable, if busy.

Since Mary is well enough to look after the new baby now, I help Mrs. Orchard with the school she holds in her home a few hours in the afternoons and Emily and George come with me. Some children stay the whole week, the weekend as well. Mrs. Orchard keeps them if they are not collected by Friday night and on those occasions Emily and George help us to amuse the children on the Saturday.

Mr. Tremayne came last Saturday to offer his services. Mrs. Orchard had a spark in her eye as she informed me that he has been helping so much more of late. I find this talk distressing, for there is no way I can marry, and someone as suitable and pleasing as Mr. Tremayne just makes that knowledge all the more painful. Mary is the only one who knows why; I am sure she has not even told Will.

Mrs. Orchard is correct in her observations of Mr. Tremayne, I believe. He is friendly with quite a few people, one of them being the Buchanan gentleman who manages the huge Anlaby property. Mr. Tremayne, in his inimitable style, had helped this gentleman at some stage with his upturned carriage and the favour has never been forgotten. It is said that the Tremayne family always has a mutton roast on Sunday. And for today, he had managed to procure an invitation to take the school children to a picnic in Anlaby grounds.

Along with Mr. and Mrs. Orchard, the party consisted of the six children (Emily and George included), Mr. Tremayne and myself. I helped Mrs. Orchard pack the picnic and we started early in Mr. Orchard's wagonette as it was all of eleven miles out. The excitement of the children was infectious and I found myself light-hearted, looking forward to the excursion. Nor were my expectations disappointed. Anlaby was a fairyland. There were people around with jobs to do, many buildings too, even with wooden slates on the roof. The house, all stone, with its terrace on three sides, was a lovely sight. It was the first time since leaving Cornwall that I had seen so many oak trees. There is a whole avenue of them, tiny yet, of course, and more besides, leading up to the house. Mr. Buchanan employs quite a few gardeners to tend the roses and little paths leading to hidden bowers. It was most delightful. There is said to be thousands upon thousands of sheep and the land stretches the same distance as from Camborne to Land's End!

We chose a rise by the dam near the house, under shady trees. We were determined to enjoy the day despite flies and other vermin; how gentle the Cornish countryside seems in recollection. Nothing to hurt one except the nettles; but even then there were dock plants provided to alleviate the suffering.

The children played while Mrs. Orchard and I set out on a rug the picnic from the baskets. Emily had insisted on wearing the new boots I had brought for her from home. With her bonnet on, pinafore over her dress and white pantaloons showing off those boots, she was a pretty sight. Adventurous George and his friend were already climbing the nearby gum trees. Boys will climb; I did not fret, and Emily stood below watching. I could hear her from a distance, admonishing him to be careful. And suddenly we heard her screams.

'What is the matter?' Mrs. Orchard was already wiping her hands on her apron.

'It's Emily,' I cried and we started down the rise to see. Soon it was all too plain. George was hanging by his little coat and one foot from a branch, his skirt up round his ears, and under him settled the murky deep water of the dam.

'Don't struggle,' I shouted above Emily's crying. 'It's all right, we're coming.' But Mr. Tremayne was there before us, hoisting himself up the trunk and climbing onto the branch. 'Hold on, Georgie lad. Keep still. I can reach you.' We all of us were hoping the branch would hold and they both wouldn't drop into the water below. With stretching out along the branch, Mr. Tremayne managed to lift the poor boy back up. But for the fright, and losing his cap in the water, George seemed none the worse for the ordeal. Emily was more distraught.

'M-Mama said I was to look after him,' she sobbed into Mr. Tremayne's waistcoat as he knelt, holding them both. Gently, I took her from him.

'You couldn't help he climbed the tree, Emily. It wasn't your fault.'

'Mama would say 'tis,' was her cry.

Mr. Tremayne raised his eyebrows at me. 'Then there's no need to worry Mama with it, is there? He is safe now.'

Emily turned grateful eyes onto him and not a tear was seen for the rest of the day. No doubt Mary still feels the loss of our brother. Just hearing Mr. Tremayne calling George 'Georgie' brought it all back to me. What a terrible time it was, though it seems to me a burden that Emily should not have to carry. I resolved also to offer to make George some trousers. He was nearly five, quite old enough to feel the indignity of being exposed upside down from a tree.

It is obvious Mr. Tremayne exhibits many tender attributes. It almost makes one feel that he could understand any affliction that could befall a person, but I do not dare test this theory. Never will I forget the way I was treated in Camborne with more than Christmas presents to show for my time spent in making a singing career. Being a non-conformist he will have narrow views, I am sure. He has even signed the Temperance Pledge. My father took us to a Wesleyan chapel too but he had liked the occasional ale when the preacher was not watching.

No, I have seen what happens to folk who have to tread a different path in Cornish society, and the same Queen rules here. It is the same society with the same rules that must not be broken. And I must pay for breaking them. I will tell Redvers Tremayne, if he becomes more attentive, that I shall never marry.

JENEFER

I'm walking up the path under the pepper tree, thinking about something Caleb said the other week when we came back from Gawler Station. When I was with Caleb again in the confines of the ute, the intolerance we encountered on the train gradually faded to another time and place. Once we were past Freeling, green hills rolled up to meet us, like dogs happy to see us home. It was such a weird sensation; I felt like I'd been away a year and I was seeing it all afresh, as if it was part of me yet I didn't have to say it was mine. I grin now as I remember kissing Caleb on the train — not exactly what Steffi would approve of, but it was as if those people forced me to make a stand. That kiss was a stamp on a document: instead of *draft* it said *final copy*.

I was just full of everything during that ride home and couldn't help saying how beautiful it all was. I shocked even myself. If the Jenefer Tremayne of January could have heard me say that she would have puked. How can we change so quickly?

Did I say home? Home was where Cedar Rise was; my old friends, where we could walk to the station and be in the city in twenty minutes, go to cinemas and coffee shops whenever we wanted. But since the fated 'train trip' Cedar

Rise is becoming blurry. That comfortable feeling of being one of the group splinters like an icicle being attacked by a pick when I remember Amy's face as she saw Caleb. Guess I'll never have that sense of *belonging* at school here either since it's only for a year. Even though Erin and her friends are polite, it's not what you'd call a 'sharing of secrets' level of relationship. I wonder if I expect too much; Ashleigh isn't 'in' either, so maybe it takes ten years. Whether the distance they keep me at (which teachers wouldn't notice by the way, or even the boys) has anything to do with Caleb I can't tell. And what if I did stop doing things with him and the girls were more chummy with me in the way I'm used to? How long would it last? And wouldn't I feel cheated that they only let me 'in' because I played by their rules? How could I respect myself?

Caleb was as happy as if I'd said I'd follow him to Mars on some expedition that only he believed in. 'It's the land.' His hands were off the wheel again, sweeping the undulating hills into his vision. It suddenly reminded me — Dad gets this passion about things too. Look how he raved on when we first came here and I couldn't care less. But that was then. BC. Before Caleb.

'This is what being Australian is all about. It's not the colour of our skins or how long we've been here, who our grandparents were. It's this feeling for the land. It's huge. When you know you belong. Like a relationship.' He looked across at me as he said 'relationship' and I felt what he meant. Not necessarily about the land – I may never have his depth of feeling for the land – but I'm beginning to understand what it is he means and I feel I'm a part of it too.

I'm still grinning as I climb the verandah steps, not realising my life's going to make another sharp turn. One I hadn't calculated on yet, though it had to happen sometime. Kate doesn't keep me in suspense.

'We know your secret, Jenfa.' Jealousy drips through the singsong lilt to her tone. Dad's there in the lounge. He doesn't waste any time either. 'What's this box Kate says you have in your room?'

My heart sinks. So Kate found it at last. This is it. No more Zenna Dare. At least no more Zenna Dare on my own terms. And what if it all gets stopped? There's not enough time to think of another History topic. They're both watching me; even the energy to be angry with Kate drains away. Steffi's putting the skillet on the stove; I hear its heavy bang through the wall. Incredible. The things that seem clear when your life is about to change. Hamilton's on the rug playing with Sher Khan. He must have got him used to being loose in the house already. Sher Khan's running, Hamilton claps his hands; the rabbit stops. I hadn't noticed him running round like this before. Life's been marching on, while I've been immersed in the nineteenth century.

I can't just tell them the box is nothing. I remember something else: Gweniver is Kate's triple-great-grandmother too. And so I climb into the cage and go down with the sharks.

'It was hidden in the room under the stairs.' I hear Kate's indrawn breath, like a steam train ready to go. Her eyes are shining. Plain excitement? Or triumph?

'Who put it there?' Dad.

'Gweniver Tremayne.'

'Can I see? Dad?' Dad ignores Kate for a bit. He's still facing me. He looks hurt. I never expected that. Anger and 'Let's look at it now'. That I expected, and I'm braced for it, but not this half-surprised, half 'Why didn't you trust me?' look.

'Dad — I just wanted to see what I could find out before I told you. So there'd be something to say. It didn't all make sense —'

'What didn't?'

'What's in the box?' They're both talking at once and Hamilton picks up Sher Khan, sits back and watches us.

'There are papers —'

'Papers?'

'Pages, really, but they're not in order, not dated. One or two are. There are a few letters too. Poems.' I have to make him understand. 'It's like a jigsaw puzzle.'

'I like jigsaw puzzles.' Kate's pouting. Dad looks as if he feels the same.

'It belongs to the family, Jenefer.'

'Yeah, not just you —' this from Kate until Dad quietens her with one of his looks. He's got a few on hand today.

I'm trying not to get teary; he can do it to me every time. 'Guess you want to see it.'

'Yes, that would be a good start, Jenefer.' The dryness of his tone hurts more than the shouting he can lash out with.

I lead the invasion down the stairs, hoping Kate hasn't

broken the wheel trying to get into the box. Oh, why wasn't there a lock on my door? I could have put a padlock on the bookcase, but that would have given the secret opening away for sure. I drag out the box. Dad helps; then kneels down. He whistles, just like Caleb. 'What a work of art!'

Then I show them how to open it and hand over the photos of Gweniver and Zenna Dare. Dad's thoughtful for a while, then, 'I can see why you kept this quiet, Jenefer. There's something here, isn't there?'

I know what he means and my breath catches suddenly. He understands! He's looking up at me again and it's not the 'I'm boss of everything' look that I'd dreaded whenever I'd envisioned this moment. He's still got the photo of Zenna Dare in his hand.

'So Gweniver had an alias?' His face is a question mark. How did he get to that so quickly? I'd always hoped, of course, right when I'd read that very first card: *Dear Zenna, why did you not come?* But I had to check out if Zenna Dare wasn't a real person so I could be sure. It would have been devastating to go down that track and find out Zenna was just a pet name after all, as Aunt Dorie thought. I nod at him, still hesitant.

'I can't prove it, but it looks like it. No one with the name of Zenna Dare was even born in Cornwall or England, let alone came out here. As far as can be found out.' A new gleam in Dad's eyes now. Interest? Respect?

'An actress?'

'Singer, I think.' And I tell him about Ginny Rivers, the music halls, the tea gardens. Show him the playbill.

Everything I know so far. 'There's something else.'

'What's that?'

How can I explain it? To me it's clear. It may not be to him, nor do I want to say every single thing in front of Big Ears Kate. 'She was sad about something.'

'How can you tell that?' I know what's he's thinking. Supposition, women's intuition. So I show him the pages I've typed already.

'It's hard to explain. A tone in the writing. Sometimes the writing is so hard to read it's like she must have been upset. She always refers to something that's happened before but doesn't spell it out. Says she'll never marry, but we know she did.' And what about the singing? Didn't she think she was born for it? Why give it up and come to Australia?

Dad looks at me a moment, like he's searching my face for clues before he glances down, and reads aloud:

Truly I do not know what to do. Old Harry Sanders, the organ grinder, seems to understand. He has a daughter my age, he said. He has been very kind to me when I have needed comfort the most. Now I shall go home, just as he suggested. I don't belong in the Music Halls and Pleasure Gardens. I thought I could do it but the cost is too great. R will not understand. I am making him a pretty penny, I think. But he has many students; he won't be devastated for long. ·

Dad looks up. 'You've done all this?' I nod.

'I haven't typed them all yet, and they're not in order.'

'You know what date this is?'

'No. It's one of the hard ones. And even the ones I've dated are not necessarily when she wrote them. Most of the Cornish ones are like she's looking back, as if she wrote them later, like an autobiography, so I reckon she wrote most of them here in Kapunda.' I show him the others where I've basically worked out the sequence. 'I know she came here in 1849, so anything written about Kapunda is going to be around then, and before 1852 when she finally married Redvers. There are a few letters which help date some of the Cornish ones. She must have started singing lessons around early 1845 because she mentions a March fair. I looked it up on the Internet — the March Fair wasn't held every year — 1845 was the closest, considering she mentions she's sixteen. And if she was Zenna Dare she was in her first production late in 1846.' I show him the page off the 'net about the Cinderella opera and *The Bohemian Girl*.

There's open admiration in Dad's face now. Even Kate has let her mouth gape. 'So it could all fit?'

I nod vigorously this time. 'And I want to find out if it's true. Dad, I'm not being morbid. Please don't tell Aunt Dorie.' I don't mention how I feel I *have* to find out. To put something right. He'd say how can you put something right after 160 years? What's done is done. Caleb says finding out something, acknowledging it, starts a process of healing. Like an open sore finally gets a scab on it — there'll always be a scar but at least it doesn't bleed anymore.

Dad's eyes narrow slightly. 'Aunt Dorie?'

'She won't understand. She thinks we should leave the past alone. You don't mind me finding out, do you?'

The hesitation is slight, enough to make me hold my breath. 'S'pose not. But I'd like to be kept posted.' Then he offers money — photocopying and expenses. I'm in the middle of saying thanks when he gets onto this obsessive thing. 'No need to spend too much time on it, Jenefer.'

It's afterwards when the kids are doing their teeth that he tells me this is Kate's and Hamilton's ancestry too. Kate's interested — is there anything I can think of that she can share in? I go down the hall to their rooms; carry Hamilton into Kate's bed and start telling them a story. About a girl called Gweniver who could play a lute and always wanted to sing. Who loved roses and words, did embroidery and literature in school and had a brother called Georgie.

After Hamilton is asleep, Kate asks me. 'I want to help, Jenfa. I like Gweniver too. She has a pretty name. Dad told me it means the same as yours.' She's slightly peeved again and I'm quick to tell her how special the name Kate is. It's when I'm vacantly gazing at her school drawings on the wall that I suddenly think of something she can do. 'How would you like to draw pictures?'

'What of?'

'Gweniver. Cornwall. The mine. You could get stuff off the web. Bet there's loads of info in your library at school about Kapunda. Cornwall too, since so many of the

147

immigrants here were Cornish.' I have every confidence in Kate's abilities. I couldn't do half the stuff at ten that she can do. Her eyes are glistening. When that happens with Kate, it's usually excitement; it rolls her forward like a train with faulty brakes going down a slope. 'Really? We could make it into a book for the family.'

That stops me short for a bit. I'm thinking History assignment but I could make another copy. 'Kate, let's keep it in the family too. We don't need the whole of Kapunda knowing about everything just yet.'

She nods wisely. *At least wait until we find out what Gweniver's secret was,* I say to myself. I get an uneasy feeling in the pit of my stomach lately that something so carefully hidden as that box had to be hidden for a good reason.

Hamilton's warm and floppy as I carry him back to his blue room. Then I go back down to mine. Dad said I could keep the box here considering I was the one who found it. It's in my bay window. No need to hide it now and I start deciphering another page.

Oh why, Gweniver? Why didn't you want to marry Redvers?

GWENIVER

I see a lily on thy brow,
  With anguish moist and fever dew;
And on thy cheek a fading rose
  Fast withereth too.

'La Belle Dame sans Merci',
John Keats 1795–1821

What could have possessed me to accept Mr. Tremayne's invitation to the ball at Anlaby last night? Even Mary encouraged me, and Mrs. Orchard; she has left no doubt as to what she thinks about it all. She even lent me a shawl and gloves. Mary has helped me make a new dress so I did not have to wear my black. It was just like years ago when we would have dances on the green at fairs on Midsummer's Day.

Mr. Tremayne had borrowed a buggy and I do believe it is the first time I have been in a vehicle like that since those jaunts with Mr. Drew and his parties in Penzance and singing in the Assembly Rooms at Truro. I must not dwell on those days and the times afterwards but often I wonder how many others he served as he served me.

I am not deserving of Mr. Tremayne's attentions, however, and I think I will have to tell him why. He seems to take no notice of hints towards that direction at all. At Anlaby last night I was torn in two. Miss Buchanan was so kind as to invite us at all; there were so many fashionable folk present including the set of young people that do many things together. If only they knew that I too had been part of such a select group.

The room underneath the house had been gaily decked out with roses and white lilacs. It was so pleasant and cool underground that it was not as much a hardship dancing in this climate as I thought it would be. I had no idea Mr. Tremayne with his chapel-going would even enjoy such an evening, yet enjoy it he did. The only difference between him and the other young men was that he did not drink the wine or punch on offer. He even danced with me although he did not hold me too closely. Mr. Tremayne is such a paradox; even though he will not touch alcohol, he has been seen walking into the Sir John Franklin public house to see a friend. Yet most other non-conformists would shun such a practice in case it was misunderstood.

Last night, he seemed so happy and young at heart. I ruined all that, of course. It was when he took me out to the gardens.

'It is so beautiful here,' I said at first. It did not quite explain the feeling I had; the moon shining, the roses scenting the air, and yes, Mr. Tremayne's charm was not wasted on me either but I had to keep guard against that. He tucked my arm through his as we made our way down the steps to the rose bower below. Even in the moonlight

I could see the whiteness of the tiny roses. They tugged at my heart long before he started speaking.

'Miss Rundle, I want to ask you something tonight.' And I felt the immediate premonition: fear. I should not have come. Yes, I should have known.

'Mr. Tremayne —' Somehow I had to put him off, change the pattern of his thoughts.

'Please — we have shared so much over the last year.' His voice was warm, caressing. How was I going to withstand him? I groaned inwardly, but of course he knew nothing of my torment. He carried on talking. 'Helping at the school, those Sabbath School picnics at the Willows.' He laughed then, remembering something, while I only grew more afraid. 'And Baker's Flat.' He turned to face me, moved in closer. 'I think that is when I was sure. Just the way you listened to the young Irish women in those dreadful hovels the mine calls cottages. The way you helped with the sick children. I haven't seen that done before except in a condescending way. I admire you greatly, Miss Rundle.' He stopped for a moment. 'No, it is more, much more. I love you. Please, I would like us — to marry. I know God can only smile upon our union.'

How could I tell him? I should be happy if circumstances were different. How gladly I would have married Redvers Tremayne, but, alas, I could not. And I said it aloud.

'I cannot. Cannot marry you. Please believe me. I am not worthy of a man of your calling.' What more could I say without spelling it out? In the dark I could imagine him frowning, heard it in his voice as he objected. 'I don't understand. What do you mean, you cannot marry me? You do not care? I thought I could see it — in the way you regarded me sometimes ...' his voice trailed away. I could not tell if it was in hurt or anger.

I moved away. 'No. It is not you.' Not you. I felt like screaming, I love you too. I will marry you regardless but will you still respect me when you find out? Will love turn to hate? I do not think I could bear the shame.

'If it is not me, what then? You have promised someone else?'

'No.'

'What can stop you? You're already married? If you're a widow, it makes no difference to me, Gweniver.' I could not bear the sudden hope in his tone, but Redvers Tremayne would always have hope. Yes, that is it, I thought. He has his faith and hope; he will survive this. But how will I?

'No. It's not like that.' Worse, I could have said, but did not. 'Please just believe me. If I could tell you, you would understand and you would despise me.'

'Never.' I felt the passion, the heat in his breath as he bent closer, actually put his hands on my arms. 'Nothing you could say would change the way I feel about you. I know you. I've seen you with children, people in need. You have a good heart. You love others — that's what true godliness is. That cannot be taken away whatever has happened in the past.'

His words almost made me laugh but it would have

been an ugly sound. Me? Godly? If only he knew. And suddenly I was crying, bitterly, silently. He could not know that the place he chose for this was too much for me to bear. Let alone the things he was saying. The scent of the roses themselves was condemning me. Those pure white blooms, seen even in the moonlight for what they were, pointing their thorns at me, mocking me.

His voice was gentle then. 'Forget about whatever you think is unworthy, Miss Rundle, I never need know. It is in the past.' I could tell from his tone that he could not imagine anything hideous in my life at all. Yet I still could not accept him. It would be a wrong against him and against his future family.

Once he realised my mind was made up, Mr. Tremayne promised not to speak of it again. After all that I had no enthusiasm left for staying the night and having a grand time, as the others had put it. Mr. Tremayne took me directly to the buggy and we drove home in silence with only the candle lantern flickering to light our way.

JENEFER

Caleb and I have decided to have our own picnic at Anlaby. Actually, I invited him. It's interesting, Caleb has never been there before and yet he's lived in the area almost all his life. As soon as I read Gweniver's account, I had to see it for myself. I've managed to get my 'L's at last and I pull up at the gate with a bit of a roar and a lurch. I think I took my foot off one of the pedals before the other. Caleb's controlling himself, which is impressive considering he has responsibility for the ute. Dad wouldn't have controlled himself like that. He took me out on the main road in the twin cab last Sunday. It was awful. He didn't explain anything properly for a start and then expected me to know what to do. I nearly crashed into a truck trying to pass me. Honestly, you can't see anything in that blind spot. When the canopy is on, the twin cab has a huge one.

The first thing I notice is the oaks; they're giants. 'These trees are still here, just like Gweniver wrote.' There's a sign: *Please park here and walk up the driveway to the house.* And another sign on the gate: *Please shut the gate.* Two huge Clydesdales stand munching a metre from the gate and stare at us as if we're the hundredth lot of people they've seen all day. They don't look hopeful that we'll leave it open either. Another stack of monster oak trees line the drive up to the house. Their trunks look like they've been rooted here for more than 160 years.

Already I can tell this place is incredible. There are ruins of garden-type outhouses. I find out later they were conservatories. There's a grotto made of cement, filled with huge cacti, an old early twentieth century swimming pool. Peacocks strutting on ancient terraced lawns.

'Look at the maypole, Caleb.' Masses of roses climb the rusty chains up to the pole in the middle. We pay our money to be part of a tour and see everything, even forty-odd carriages and coaches. I get a kick out of seeing carriages with 1850 or earlier written on cards beside them. I wonder if Gweniver rode in one like this. Or this: *Cobb & Co, an original.* Straining, I peek into the window of *Queen Emma's Barouche from Holland.* And only candles went into the lamps. Caleb's not quite as interested as I am in European memorabilia; he walks around with his hands in his ripped jeans pockets, just a quick smile every now and then.

We even get shown the underground ballroom, now made into a flat. I mention Gweniver. The lady who lives here now is kind, willing to help. I feel the immediate coolness, almost dampness as we step down. See the dark wood round the edges of the room, beautiful lamps, chequered windows. *Gweniver and Redvers came here, danced here. Why wasn't she happy that night?*

We go out again, onto an underground verandah, then

up to the main level. This verandah has Victorian tiles like the ones at school — diamonds, maroon, black, cream — and looks out onto the varying levels of poplars, and all the trees that have been planted over the last 160 years. Italian pillars hold up the verandah; majestic steps guide the eye to the green shutters on the windows. The wind reaches down suddenly through the poplars out there; they shake and shine like silver pennies in the sun, glinting and whispering. They make me want to go down to find out what they know. The fountain looks like it hasn't worked for fifty years and I wonder if it was there when Gweniver was. Probably not.

Caleb brightens up as we head down to the dam. We sit on the grass with half-cold hamburgers while I wonder if this is the dam that Gweniver came to that day. Odd feeling, standing where you know your ancestors walked. We walk all round the dam, holding hands, not saying much. Then Caleb thinks of this idea. 'You go hide. I'll find you.'

I laugh. 'Okay. But we don't go through any gates alone — otherwise we'll never find each other.' We agree on the terms. He lies down and closes his eyes while I wrench myself away to find an accommodating bush. It's hilarious watching him find me. It doesn't take long; apparently I've left tell-tale clues.

'All right. We go through this gate, then you hide.' After counting to a hundred I walk through a paddock with another dam, looking behind every tree, until I come across him, sitting grinning behind a huge eucalypt, picking his teeth with a twig. 'Why aren't you hiding?'

'Thought you'd find me sooner or later. May as well just sit here.'

'That's not fair. We'll go through this gate and I'll really hide.' I know we'll be in the garden then. I undo the orange twine round the gate; tie it up again. 'Ready?' He's got this look on his face, like *What will I get when I find you?* I run off. *Find me first, Caleb, then we'll see.* But when I get into the ancient rose garden, I falter.

There's a Grecian statue that most probably wasn't there when Gweniver was, but the roses sure look ancient. All with little signs on, giving botanical names. Hedges, bushes, stray grass; the poplars murmuring high above. Ghost gums whispering secrets, like waves crashing on rocks in the far distance. Did they hear Redvers? What bitter disappointment he must have felt that night, yet Gweniver wrote nothing of how it must have affected him.

I go down some steps onto a grassy terrace; find a spot in the rose bower where white roses are climbing over an archway; lie down and close my eyes. The peacocks from the other side of the gardens call out, and a bird answers close by. Honestly, when you close your eyes in a place like this it sounds like the sea pulling back after rolling up on the sand.

I feel Caleb's shadow on me before I hear him. 'You're no challenge.' I squint up at him and grin as he sits down.

'You know, Caleb, do you ever get a sense of people being here before? I don't just mean here, but in places where you go?'

'Sometimes, I guess.' He's picking blades of grass; puts one between his teeth.

'I really feel it here. They walked, talked here. If only words stayed in the atmosphere and you could catch them years later — feel them in the air.'

'You mightn't like that if everyone could do it. What if people weren't happy? What if there was killing? We wouldn't want to hear the screams forever.'

I can see his point and we fall quiet. This is like a secret garden, a jungle overgrown. How many secrets are hidden here? How many people came to propose? How much happiness? Sadness too, like Caleb said.

What was Gweniver trying to tell Redvers that night? He proposed; she cried. Why? I know she wasn't married before — her name was still Rundle. Because she'd been on the stage? A singer? Why should it matter anyway?

'So what has today done for you?'

I don't answer straight away. I still don't know what Gweniver's problem was, nor do I really expect to find out. 'It's just been good to be here where they were,' I say. At least Caleb understands this. He grunts in agreement and moves closer to claim his reward for finding me. It's not until I get home that I realise what I put Caleb through. So much land that belonged to one English family years ago, just like any farm or station in this state, but not only my ancestors walked on it — his might have too.

Later, when I check my mail, there's an answer from the Cornish library. They were quicker than I expected.

From: Royal Cornish Library
To: Jenefer Tremayne
Subject: Zenna Dare

Dear Jenefer Tremayne

There were a number of theatres in Cornwall in the early 19th century. Here in Truro we had the Assembly Rooms. This building survives and was the venue for social events such as balls as well as theatre. Contemporary newspapers would have some information although we have no index for this subject as yet.

There is a good book, Music in Cornwall by R. Hammat, Exeter: University of Exeter Press, 1992. It's not an e-book but you may be able to access it through a library.

I hope the above details will be of some help.

Sincerely yours
Lisa Rowse

From: Jenefer Tremayne
To: State Library, South Australia
Subject: Cornish Resource

Dear Information Manager

I see that you do not have the following title available on your catalogue:

Music in Cornwall by R. Hammat, Exeter: University of Exeter Press, 1992.

Is there some way of getting it from another library?

Thank you, Jenefer Tremayne

GWENIVER

Dearest Gweniver

I hope this letter finds you well enough. Clarice wrote immediately of your misfortune and I am writing by return ship. My dear Gweniver, all is not lost. Not if you come as soon as you can, immediately you receive this. Will and I have been able to build a cottage. I think you would like life out here. You always did take more risks; I would never have been brave enough to go all the way to Penzance for those singing lessons, though look at me coming to the colonies with Will. Who would have thought I would be brave enough to do something like this?

Life here has its compensations, even excitements, apart from the lack of art and history and refined society. But who cares about all that? Did we when we were young? Perhaps you did. But you would be surprised how we still have social gatherings here. There is even a theatre in Adelaide, though we have never been.

Will and I are making a good life. He earns much more than he ever did in Wheal South Crofty and now that there is copper here in Kapunda and in Burra Burra too, the colony is much more prosperous. There are no taxes like at home, many things are expensive but meat is only threepence a pound. Can you imagine? Though I keep a lock on the tea tin.

There is quite a Cornish community here now, even a Bible Christian Chapel (though we meet in a home at present) and many fine folk attend. In that respect life is much as it was at home. Some English folk call us the howling Methodists, but they are not vindictive. There are opportunities, some jobs even. Many fine single men have come with their parents. There are not enough single ladies as most come married.

We would be very happy for you to come and live with us. Since the birth of George I have not been so well. Oh, Gweniver, I miss the way we talked and helped at all the chores when we were younger. I have no one to help me here. We have not had butter for so long as I do not have the strength, and there is no woman to lend a hand.

Will is very busy. He is saving his tribute to buy more land. There is no shortage of land here. It seems the natives never used it.

Oh, I do pray you will come.

Your ever loving sister

Mary

JENEFER

Everyone at school has been hyped about the Celtic Festival. Erin and Tim, Caleb and I are going together. Tim is Caleb's mate so since Erin's been going out with him we've been on a few doubles down at the footy clubrooms. The cinema at Gawler too, with tea at an Italian cafe first. Last week we went up to Tea Tree Gully. Sometimes we just hang around the cafes down the street. What Kapunda needs is a cinema complex.

There are still a few doors Erin hasn't let me through. It's weird because she'll tell me stuff about her and Tim but I sense a slight disapproval when I mention Caleb. Tim isn't snobby like Ben Walker and he's nicer in some ways to me than Erin is, when you consider what Erin doesn't talk to me about. Like yesterday, she and I saw Caleb down the street with his three smallest cousins, buying them ice-creams. Guess Amy would pronounce that as so uncool, but even though Erin's not like Amy or Alicia, I could tell she still noticed but pretended not to. Can't work out what her problem is. Caleb's got something even different from Tim — wish Erin could see it — soul, I think musicians call it.

This weekend because of the festival all the kids are

staying in the town. Big-name music groups are coming from Europe even. I'd never been into country music much and I always thought Celtic music was much the same but it's not at all. And Caleb let out a big secret of his own. Actually it was Tim.

'So, getting your guitar out for the festival?'

Caleb looks sheepish as I say, 'What?' How can you miss something like that about someone when you've known them over three months?

Tim's not embarrassed, however. 'Yeah. Caleb's a cool dude on the strings. Aren't you, mate?' While Caleb's telling him to bloody well shove it.

'What's wrong?' I'm saying. 'Playing the guitar is cool, isn't it? Why didn't you tell me before?'

'I'm not that good,' Caleb mutters.

'Not that good' turns out to be better than some. It's Saturday of the festival and we're at the Clare Castle Hotel at a jam session for Celtic musicians. Caleb's joined in as well as a few others I remember seeing at school. There're these really old guys too who belong to a Celtic music club in Adelaide. One's so cute — he's even made his own concertina. Some play tin whistles, violins, flutes; there's a woman with a brilliant voice who sounds like she's come off a mermaid's rock. Sometimes a few of the guys sing too. I even hear Caleb join in on some of the old ballads.

The Castle Hotel is so old — rock walls and red velvet curtains — and the happy, beery atmosphere makes me feel like we're in the nineteenth century. Already I'm clapping,

Caleb's stamping if he's not playing. Between songs I lean over. It must be the feeling of goodwill in the air, why I can joke with him. 'How come you're playing white-fella music, Caleb?'

He takes it as the joke it's intended to be, but I'm not ready for his answer. He grins. 'Dad was Irish.'

'Irish?' For a second I'm floored, then I catch on. Irish like my dad's Cornish. Me too, now I think about it.

'He loved music. It's not often I get into it like this, but when I do I wonder why I don't do it more often.'

I must be still staring at him.

'What? You think I'd only be playing didgeridoos?'

I wouldn't have put it exactly like that, but it is a thought. Why doesn't he do music at school? The next song starts and he leans closer so I can hear. 'Only black fellas up north play them.' Then he grins again. 'This one plays guitar.'

He's gentle with me but it's a lesson I don't think I'll ever forget. Stereotyping, underestimating. There must be so many words for it. Even I had begun to put Caleb in a box. And Caleb is one person who doesn't fit well in a box of anyone's making.

Caleb's singing again, grinning at me. It's a Celtic love song about a witchy girl called Maggie May. With a voice like an angel's lay. Incredible. All that music on his CDs in the ute, his singing along. And I never guessed that he played himself. His voice isn't bad either. The things you find out about people. I laugh and try to join in.

It's Caleb who puts the seed in my head the next day. 'If your grandmother could sing and she lived here in Kapunda, wouldn't people have known about it?' He always refers to Gweniver as my grandmother, as if the greats don't matter. As though the dead and alive are all part of the one living family.

I'm thinking of how it took me three months to find out he could play guitar. 'Bet they didn't have Celtic Festivals. How would anyone know?'

'Come with me. I'll show you something.' He takes me to the window of the antique shop. 'Look at that.'

There's a whole display of musical artefacts from the nineteenth century. Put out for the Festival obviously.

'This is excellent.' I'm looking at the instruments: tin whistles, a concertina just like the one the musician played last night at the Castle Hotel, ancient, though. A small organ. Then I see it. A playbill. Not unlike the one in Gweniver's box.

POSITIVELY FOR TWO NIGHTS ONLY.

Tuesday 29th

&

Wednesday 30th June 1865

GREAT ATTRACTION

held in

CRASE'S ASSEMBLY ROOM.

The popular and celebrated artist

EDITH PALMERTON

(Mrs. W. Alexander)

assisted by Mr. W. Alexander
will appear in her

MUSICAL AND MIMICAL ENTERTAINMENT:

HOUSEHOLD SKETCHES.

With original characters and elaborate costumes.

As given for FIVE HUNDRED NIGHTS
in London, Liverpool and recently at
White's Assembly Rooms, Adelaide.

Admission — reserved seats 4s, unreserved 2s.

DOORS OPEN AT HALF PAST SEVEN,

TO COMMENCE AT EIGHT O'CLOCK.

I wonder what 'mimical' meant. Was it a real concert or a pretend one? Impersonators, like Elvis Presley and Tina Turner lookalikes? Some people make a whole living out of it. 'Maybe if they had such things in 1865, Gweniver might have sung in them.'

Caleb's walking inside.

'Where are you going?'

'If anyone knows, the lady here will. She helps all the kids on their History projects.' He doesn't make History projects sound like a bad thing anymore and I follow him willingly through a forest of restored furniture to the desk. I must tell Steffi; she could sell her pieces here.

'Hi, Caleb.' The lady knows him well. She looks at me with her forehead all crinkled and Caleb introduces me. 'This is Jenefer Tremayne.' Then her eyes flicker with interest. 'You're the Tremayne family that's moved back?' It's an interesting way of putting it. She's the first person who has. Not, 'You're the new family that's moved in', but moved back, like we belonged here in the first place. It's the first time I dare to think I might actually learn to fit in here. Maybe Dad was right about us and Kapunda. When you think about it, it was Gweniver and Redvers who set it up for me. Who knows, the Tremaynes may have been here longer than Erin's family. It's a new thought and it almost makes me grin as I return the woman's look with her same amount of warmth. 'Are you interested in history, like Caleb, Jenefer?'

I look back at Caleb. Caleb? History? Maybe she means

his mother. He's grinning as usual. So I nod at her. 'Then you'll know all about the house your family built?' I nod again. 'And your great-grandfather Albert who went to the Boer War?'

'No.'

'And World War One — he's on our war memorial. You haven't seen it?'

I shake my head. 'How do you know?'

'It's my business.'

'She's a historian,' Caleb cuts in with a grin at the woman. She's not so old either; what's more, I can tell she's fond of Caleb.

'Actually, another side of your family made enquiries and I had to do research for them. The Davies.'

'Davies?'

'Honour Davies married Albert Tremayne.'

'Um, I'm more interested in Redvers and Gweniver Tremayne. He was the first —'

'Ah, the one who built the Manse.'

'Yes. Do you know anything about them? Like if she sang or anything? There's a playbill in your window. Is there more stuff like that?'

'I haven't researched them at all.' For a second I'm disappointed; in the next second, glad. Glad that I'm breaking new ground. It's fun finding things out for yourself, even more fun that no one else knows yet.

'But you can easily find out.'

'How?' I cut in before she can draw breath.

'The library has the *Kapunda Herald* on CD.'

'That's the newspaper,' Caleb whispers.

'Thanks.' I can't get out of there quickly enough. Not before the lady says she'd like a copy of what I write up in case other family members ask in the future. Other family members? She makes it sound like there're a thousand of us. And besides, how much will be suitable for the public eye?

Caleb leaves me in the library while he goes to find Tim and Erin. Right now, I don't even care about the band from Europe that's playing in the street. I can hear them anyway with their high-powered PA system that makes my heart thump. Good thing the information office, museum and library are open. They must know people come on days like today to check up on family history. Fortunately, no one's thought of *The Herald* and I insert the disk in the drive. Amazing not having stuff like this available online but it would take ages to key it in, I guess. I take my iPad from my bag for writing notes and wait for the old newspaper to load. This is going to be one huge job. *The Herald* started way back in 1864. Each issue had four pages but they're so big. The columns are unending. Such tiny print. How on earth did they read it? All the ads are on the first page. Really boring ones about boots and Holloway's pills — the best thing for all ailments from weakness to asthma. Latest news from England (ha, bet that was four months old), murder on the road, housewife's corner. I skip through a lot of it until I get to May and see another playbill.

SIXPENNY
ENTERTAINMENTS

in aid of
KAPUNDA INDUSTRIAL AND
ART EXHIBITION

Will be held in the Institute Hall, Kapunda
THIS FRIDAY EVENING, MAY 7TH.

PROGRAMME

Overture... ...	Mrs. Tremayne
Song... ...	Mr. Black
Glee... ...	Mr. W. Hawke & party
Song......	Miss Batten
Violin Recital...	Mr. Williams

INTERVAL

Overture... ...	Mrs. Tremayne
Duet... ...	Mr. Black &
	Miss E. Tremayne
Song... ...	Miss Noack
Glee... ...	Mr. W. Hawke & party
Song... ...	Miss Christmas

Admission 6d.

DOORS OPEN AT 7.30 P.M.

COMMENCE AT 8 O'CLOCK.

Mrs Tremayne. It has to be Gweniver. She said she wouldn't be able to stop singing. But what if Redvers' mother sang? Does 'Mrs Tremayne' prove anything? They had big families; it could be anyone. I keep searching. Then in November of the same year I see the following: an article so small I almost miss it, in tiny print that's hard to read. I print a copy.

KAPUNDA HERALD

1864, November 17th

Two hundred pounds were raised at last week's charity function at Crase's Assembly Room. Mrs. Redvers Tremayne delighted the audience with her rendition of ballads from the old country. Her daughters, Miss Emmelene Tremayne and Miss Mary Jayne Tremayne sang a duet while nine-year-old twins, Masters Percy and Nathan Tremayne played fiddles to accompany them. It is obvious that even the younger Tremaynes have musical gifts. Usually, Mrs. Tremayne and the children have confined their talents to Sunday Worship at the Bible Christian Chapel and Sabbath School. All have agreed on what a treasure-trove Mr. Tremayne has been hiding in his home. We hope Mrs. Tremayne will consent to sing at another community function, of which we have many here in Kapunda.

If Gweniver was trying to hide her secret, I reckon I've caught her out. If only the people knew they had the real thing. She obviously never told anyone she'd been on the stage in London. That's if I'm right and she was Zenna Dare. Wish I could prove it, but how?

Suddenly Caleb's here, hanging over my shoulder. 'You finished?'

'I don't know.' Would this ever be finished? There must be clues everywhere. Most probably her name is mentioned more times in the paper, but I wouldn't know where to look since it's not indexed. Caleb's breathing heavily and I look up at him, worried.

'What's wrong?'

Then he gives this slow grin. 'Nothing's wrong. Something else I want to show you. Can you come now?'

He's not usually so pushy. But it is the Festival after all. I should go out and enjoy it with him. I give back the CD with thanks to the volunteer and Caleb's fairly pulling me out of the door and leading me down the street, past stalls that have been set up for the festivities. There are quite a few of them: Celtic stalls with DVDs and CDs, Celtic crosses.

Another artist is singing now in the street, Jeanette Wormald. Caleb has said he likes her Australian sound. 'She understands the land,' he'd said that time. 'She walks gently on it.' And I stand to listen, but I get pulled further along. Camels, led by an old guy in long baggy clothes, taking kids for rides. That must be Caleb's boss. An actor dressed as a woman, squirting water on everyone from a briefcase; a town crier; a Scottish pipe band tuning up; archers in green straight from Sherwood Forest; an organ grinder. Organ grinder? I stop short a second. I wonder if Gweniver's friendly organ grinder was like this one: a man in European breeches and white shirt, turning the handle on this huge wooden organ with little brass pipes on the front, beating out 'De Camptown Ladies Sing Dis Song'. He looks cheery too, as though I could go up and he'd give me a turn on the handle. But my hand gets tugged until we're standing in front of a long trestle full of antique crystal glasses, old china, clocks and photographs. Photographs. I've never seen so many before — all in folders, some for varying amounts of money. Some of famous people, another box of ordinary ones. I flick through the folders, glancing at Caleb. He's got this weird look on his face, like he's set up a treasure hunt, knows where the chocolate is and can't wait until I sniff it out. Can't imagine him wasting his time looking at European antiques. And photos that have nothing to do with him.

'How come? You're not interested in this sort of thing?'

'You are.' *You're special to me, Jenefer.* I hear it in his tone. He couldn't have been plainer.

I keep flitting, Caleb even helps, the slow grin still on his face; gives me another folder to look through. He must have known, seen it himself and then come to get me. I'm halfway through the folder when I freeze. A beautiful face, framed by a hat with flowers, looks out at me. She's in white, an off-the-shoulder neckline with lace all around it; smiling. She's ravishing, and she's Zenna Dare. It has an inscription: 'Miss Zenna Dare as Amina in La Sonnambula'. Talk about serendipity, as Dad would say! Steffi would call it divine intervention. Another opera — it has to be. I look at the cover of the folder: All five dollars in this folder, and I'm fumbling as I get my money out of my jeans pocket. Five dollars for another clue; it's cheap.

I'm holding my breath as the lady behind the stall wraps it in purple tissue paper and hands it over. Then I turn excited eyes onto Caleb. 'You are going to have an ice-cream. What would you like? Five scoops? Chocolate sauce?'

'Whew. I should find you photos every day, eh?' Then he leans closer. 'A double sounds great.' I grin; Caleb has this way of saying stuff indirectly, so it doesn't hurt your feelings. Erin calls it beating about the bush. I call it being tactful. I order two double ice-creams, chocolate and vanilla.

From: State Library South Australia
To: Jenefer Tremayne
Subject: Cornish Resource

Dear Ms Tremayne

The National Library has shown that the resource you mentioned is available from the Baillieu Library at Melbourne University. It will cost $15 for an inter-library loan, and you will be able to use it here for two weeks. Please notify us if you would like to proceed.

Yours sincerely

Lee Hutchinson

Reference Librarian

From: Jenefer Tremayne
To: State Library
Subject: Cornish resource

Dear Mr Hutchinson
Yes, please order the book re Cornish music in 19th
century for me.
Thank you
Jenefer Tremayne

It's late — I'm sitting in front of the computer, waiting
for my web browser to manifest itself. Honestly, I feel like
there are tunnels and tunnels, with twists and turns, all
connected, like an underground mine, a whole universe
of knowledge on the 'net. It's aptly named. I could find
anything, if I only had the time and knew how to access
it properly. Every time I log on there's something new, or
something I didn't try before. This time is no exception.
This time, I find someone's personal theatre site — with
old reviews scanned in.

ILLUSTRATED LONDON NEWS

LA SONNAMBULA

Her Majesty's Theatre,
London, 1847

"The Somnambulist" is the name of Bellini's
new opera this season. Bellini's music has
delighted the crowds as has the light-hearted
love story with its wronged heroine, Amina,

played by Miss Zenna Dare.

Miss Dare's singing and acting are of a high order in the opera, but far more compelling is her aura on the boards. It is beyond an audience's loftiest expectations. Never has this writer seen a portrayal of a virginal character such as Amina performed so truly and to such perfection. Miss Dare's other-worldly rendering of the sleep-walking scene high above the stage held the whole audience spellbound as indeed, dare I say, the actors below as well.

Such angelic features, clothed in Amina's vestal white, are upheld, it is said, by an equally charming goodness off the boards. Her voice has a quality which sets her apart, suggesting woodland freshness, undefiled. When one is listening to Miss Dare and closes one's eyes for a moment, one is instantly transported to the moors and fields with the wind sweeping one's hair and the scent of forest flowers in one's nostrils.

The spiteful Elvino, played by Miss Ginny Rivers, was excellently cast, but unfortunately comparison with Miss Dare in the leading role will always throw a shadow over other worthy players. Miss Rivers is another of Mr Richard Drew's students and will no doubt make a profitable living if given leading roles away from singers of the calibre of Miss Dare.

You'd think Steffi wouldn't have approved of me starting a relationship in Year 12, with all this work to do. Erin reckons her mum is onto her all the time about spending too much time with Tim. But Steffi doesn't seem to mind at all — says at least Caleb gets me out of the house. My problem was not with getting my work done, but whether I'd get too worried over it. Now, of course, it's Zenna Dare Steffi's concerned about. She thinks I'm obsessing. Can't think why.

'Do you think you're spending too much time on it, Jenefer?' This is her latest, and I can tell when it's coming. She starts first on how my assignments are going et cetera, et cetera. The conversation gets around to Zenna Dare sooner or later, because half my work this semester is based on her. I just hope she doesn't say anything to Dad. I can placate Steffi, but if Dad comes down like a wooden beam, I've had it. So has Zenna Dare.

Caleb came with me for a drive after school today. Dad was home early so we took the twin cab. I don't get in half the trouble driving with Caleb as I do with Dad. It always feels like Dad's sitting there (hanging on, his right foot forever jerking towards an imaginary brake pedal) brooding, waiting for me to stuff up. Don't get me wrong — Dad's okay, and we have lots of fun times together — but driving lessons turn him into a troll.

When we drive past the cemetery, I stop. It's so cool

when you're the one driving — you get to say where you want to go without feeling like you're putting people out. Caleb's always so accommodating, but I get guilty sometimes. The cemetery is wild. Another thing I can tell Caleb's not so keen on, so I don't take too long. It would take days to comb through the whole place but I do find Mary and Will's plot. A little girl is next to them, Anne Marie, three years, died 1853. Her little grave has this ironwork fence around it — it looks like the sides of her cot, as though she'll feel safe, just sleeping in her bed. It stops me short, for I know she must have been Mary's new baby that Gweniver wrote about. Tombstones take on a new meaning when you know something about the people. They wouldn't have been much different from us, living, loving; just doing their best.

In some ways our journeys are the same, Gweniver's and mine; we both came to Kapunda from a different place, both must have felt the anger and sadness at having to come, and if Mary's letter is anything to go by, Gweniver had no more choice than I did. Except it would have been so much worse for her. This is still my country, I was born here and I can visit where I came from if I want. How cut off she must have felt. How dark in the beginning until she made friends, got used to things. When would she ever have called herself Australian? Maybe never — Federation didn't happen for another fifty years. I wonder how I would have coped in such a 'new' and alien land like this must have seemed to her.

And then I see Rebekah Tremayne, five-month-old daughter of Gweniver and Redvers, died 1860. *The angels have taken you home, but we shall meet again.*

Caleb comes up behind me, stands there. His shadow falls on the stone. I can't move; there's so much grief in this place. So much Gweniver had to deal with. Was this why she was so sad? I'm blinking, trying to get rid of the blurriness before I turn around but Caleb pretends not to notice. Some guys would tease, or try to make a joke of it. I don't feel up to that right now and it's like he knows. I think that's the part of Caleb I enjoy the most — the way he tries to understand.

GWENIVER

North Kapunda, 1851

Wilt thou forgive that sinne where I begunne,
Which was my sin, though it were done
before?
Wilt thou forgive those sinnes, through which I
runne,
And do run still: though still I do deplore?
When thou hast done, thou hast not done,
For, I have more.

'A Hymne to God the Father',
John Donne 1572–1631

True to his word, Mr. Tremayne has not mentioned that subject again. He still helps at Sabbath School and even at Mrs. Orchard's if many children have been left at the weekend. Nothing has changed and he has not tried to keep away from me. He is pleasant to me at chapel and I am sure everyone assumes he is courting me. And I grow fonder of him every time I see him. Is this his resolve? That he will become indispensable to me? That I will change my mind? If only it was just a change of mind that was needed. Perhaps if I write it all down (and burn it later, of course), I could see it in perspective. Mr. Tremayne cannot possibly understand what is at stake, could he? What if it does not matter to him?

After that terrible night at Anlaby when I was supposed

to be so happy, I tried to tell him again. But of course, I could not spell it out. There is no way something so hideous can be discussed politely. Why was he so obtuse? It was as if he refused to understand, kept saying nothing would make a difference. He said my name, my first name, so gently: 'Gweniver. Let it go. Whatever it is. It is forgiven.' And I said he would not forgive me if he knew. He was quiet, regarding me, then I think he gave me one of his sermons. 'Who am I, Miss Gweniver, not to forgive you something that God has already forgiven? Why did Jesus Christ die on that cross if our society is forever going to keep accounts and hold others in judgement? He died for love — love of us so we don't have to live with shocking guilt, don't have to carry burdens he has said he'd willingly take.'

He was meaning my guilt. Yes, I am guilty. I did not even say that aloud. It was as though he heard me though. 'Gweniver. Let this go. Give it to God. Do not concern yourself with what I will think.'

It all sounded very well, and Mr. Tremayne was passionate in his plea, but how can I be sure he would hold to his faith if he knew about me? Men are very loving and gracious when they think all one has done is disobey one's parents or make some simple mistake.

And what if my mistake does matter to him? I cannot think of any man I know who would not be affected by it. Why should he be any different? And I need to know. But if I told him I might even lose this friendship which I am beginning to enjoy and rely on. If I lost that as well, and his respect, which is now mine, I do not think I could endure it at all.

JENEFER

It's Caleb's idea. He has to babysit Nancy, one of his cousins, so we take Kate and Hamilton as well and drive out to The Pines. Caleb has the drinks and chips and I've brought homemade pizza. I just felt like showing off my pizza. Dad reckons it's better than Pizza Hut. I've never been here before and Caleb's happy showing me around. It's really a reserve, used to be called Taylor's Gap once upon a time.

'All these pine trees were planted in the 1880s, I think. Before that this place was a sheep run. Taylor's most probably.' He grins as he says the last bit. 'They had a school here, houses. A little settlement.'

'How come you know so much?'

Kate bursts his bubble. 'It's on the sign outside the fence.'

Caleb just spreads his hands as if to say, 'Hey, I try' while I belt him with the rug.

'Come on. Let's follow the trail.'

It's a lot of fun. The track is really narrow; we pass under this squeaky branch, rubbing on its neighbour in the breeze. A kookaburra shouts out hello and other birds answer.

'Hey. What's this?' Kate's found a derelict building, half

buried. Nancy's been here before, obviously. 'It's an old pumping house.'

I stare at all the half-submerged underground pipes; marvel at what the early settlers had to go through to get water to their land.

Then there are squeals as we come to the reservoir and the kids splash each other. Brrr. I feel chilly just watching them. Kate and Nancy look cute playing together, black and red pony tails flopping in unison as they run in and out of the shallows.

'So big,' I murmur. I only expected a lake like Davidson Reserve in the town. Caleb and I put the rug down and watch the kids. No point getting the lunch out until they ask. It's one of those lazy, sunny, but not too warm autumn days. It doesn't take the kids long to remember the pizza.

Hamilton seems happier than usual. Caleb notices. We're watching him scoffing his pizza like any kid would, not in the careful way he usually does everything. We should bring him here more often. Though it's most probably not just The Pines that's doing it. Kate has been nicer to him ever since last Tuesday. It was nearly tea time; he was calling for Sher Khan in the house. The rabbit actually comes when he calls now. Hamilton's spent a lot of time training him. Kate had taken Sher Khan to the computer room while she was searching for stuff on the 'net. But she not only hadn't put him back, she had deliberately shut the door so he couldn't get out when Hamilton called. When Hamilton finally found him he just burst — no other way to describe it. One moment he was this usual kid in pyjamas, the next moment he was like one of those Monty Python segments where the top of the guy's balloon head blows off, spewing volcano ash all over the room. Kate has treated him much more carefully ever since.

'How's Zenna?' Caleb breaks in on my thoughts. He's not making fun of me; he most probably thought that's what I'd be thinking about. I usually am. Steffi's had a few more talks with me lately about my 'obsessing'. But at least I still do things with Caleb. Trying to include Kate as well, like Dad said. Things like that seem to pay off; Kate sticks up for me more now. The kids run off again and I produce a piece of paper.

'What do you make of this?' Caleb's looking at me as he takes it. Whether he's interested or not, at least he seems committed to making an effort because of me. He reads it through:

North Kapunda, 1852

I have missed Mr. Tremayne's presence so much. I had not thought he would be the sort to chase gold like other men and Mrs. Orchard cannot imagine why he went while he had so much here. I suppose she meant our relationship. What a jest. I have never given him any indication that there will be a life for us to share, so he had nothing to stay here for. Many of the single men are not returning. Some have found gold, I hear, and they are staying in Bendigo, even to marry. This place is so forlorn. Shops are deserted, buildings unfinished, farms abandoned. Only four miners stayed to work the pumps to prevent the flooding in the shafts.

Ever since Redvers Tremayne has gone I have been searching my soul. What would be worse? Living without him? Or living with him and he finds out what happened? I cannot stand this anymore. What if he does not return? Then I have wasted my life yet again. If he does return, I am going over to his house myself, the instant he gets back and have it out properly.

Caleb purses his lips. 'She was certainly screwed up.'

'What do you mean?' I can feel the hackles rise on the back of my neck.

'Wasted my life again …' Is she referring to this other problem you can't work out?'

I nod. 'She sounds like Tess in our English novel. It's so weird. If I didn't know better …'

Caleb cuts in quicker than he normally does. 'What happened to this Tess?'

'She got seduced. Nice girl, didn't know what he was doing at first and then it was too late. Couldn't stop him.'

'Date rape?'

'Guess so, but she thought she was the guilty one, not

him. He was the sleaze but she took the whole rap for it. When she realised she was pregnant she wished she was dead because no one in those days would understand she hadn't invited it. People would only look at the evidence. She was a "fallen woman" even though she felt the remorse that a good girl of that time would feel ...' My voice trails away. Caleb's staring at me. He has a totally weird expression on his face, and the words from his mum's story suddenly come back to me: they were the palest of that whole mob ... Oh Caleb, so much sadness in people's lives and we never know.

'Go on.'

'Tess lost the baby. Met another guy but when she told him she'd been seduced, he wouldn't have anything to do with her. Said she was a different person now from what he thought.'

'What crap. Everyone thought like that then? This is the nineteenth century, right?'

'Yep.'

'And Gweniver was alive then too?'

'She was earlier.'

'So it would be worse for her.'

'You're not suggesting —'

'It fits. What could be more terrible in those days than moral shame, as you say?'

'But I've read most of her papers — she isn't the type. She won't even marry Redvers because she thinks she's not good enough. She's humble, good; strong too. She survived whatever the crisis was.' Listen to me, now I'm talking about Gweniver as though she's still alive, like Caleb does.

'And what do you think the crisis was?' I'm silent.

Caleb's insistent. 'Why would she think she wasn't good enough?'

'She was from a poor family?' It sounds lame, even to me, nor do I believe it.

'What was Redvers?'

'A miner.'

Caleb grins, 'They weren't too far above the Nungas, eh?'

'Maybe because he was in the church.'

'Now we're getting somewhere. Why would a woman think she's not good enough for a guy in the church?'

And I force myself to say it. 'Because she thinks she's a sinner? She's done something unforgivable.'

'And what would that be, pray?' Caleb exaggerates, making it sound like something out of *Sense and Sensibility*. I feel like crying and I don't know why. Guess I don't want something so horrible to have happened to Gweniver. In those days it would have been dreadful. People looking at her in more disgust than those people looked at me on the train that day. From what I know of her she'd have to have been seduced like Tess. She would never have slept with someone willingly. Not the way she was brought up, not the way she wrote. And suddenly all these bits from my Tess essay come flooding into my mind: Tess did avoid Angel Clare, just like Gweniver tried to avoid Redvers. Tess thought she was unworthy too. 'Never could she conscientiously allow any man to marry her now'. You were one person, now you are another, Angel Clare had said. Is that what Gweniver felt like too?

'Jenefer, if you've read a book like this in English, didn't you ever think of it?'

I shook my head. 'I didn't want to. I thought it might be because she was on the stage. That was a big enough no-no in those days. For all we know she never even told her family she got to sing in London.'

'Providing she was Zenna Dare, right?'

I try not to let his comment upset me; I'm determined to hang onto Zenna Dare. I remember some of the comments Gweniver made about Richard Drew. She was wary of him. Even in the beginning. It all fits. I still hope she and not Ginny Rivers was Zenna Dare.

But I have no more time to think about it for just then the girls run up crying out for hide-and-seek. 'Nancy says you play with her. Can we play?'

'Please, Caleb,' Nancy presses. Even Hamilton turns up, a step behind, looking hopeful, and pleased at being included.

On the way home, with Hamilton nodding off in the back, and the girls quiet at last, Caleb says another of his astounding comments about the land around us. 'Just look at it undulating. The shape of the mounds, the little valleys.' His hands show me what he means. 'There's something so feminine about it. Don't you think?'

It's a new thought. 'Is that why people call it Mother?'

He grins across at me. It makes me feel I've understood him; guess everyone likes that feeling. 'Could be,' is all he says.

GWENIVER

NORTH KAPUNDA, 1852

Sweet day, so cool, so calm, so bright,
The bridal of the earth and sky:
The dew shall weep thy fall tonight;
For thou must die.

Sweet rose, whose hue angry and brave
Bids the rash gazer wipe his eye,
Thy root is ever in its grave,
And thou must die.

Sweet spring, full of sweet days and roses,
A box where sweets compacted lie;
My music shows you have your closes,
And all must die.

Only a sweet and virtuous soul,
Like a seasoned timber, never gives;
But though the whole world turn to coal,
Then chiefly lives.

'Virtue', George Herbert 1593–1633

Redvers Tremayne has returned, even earlier than I had hoped. But he has had an accident. I feared I had left it too late. The mail cart overturned on him just outside Kapunda near the River Light when the river came down in flood and washed away the horses and the four other passengers.

'Tis a mercy he was not also drowned. Mr. William Hawke's newly arrived brother, Nathaniel, had been coming back from Adelaide with supplies to start up butchering; he came across the horse first, then found Redvers lying on the track and brought him back. There was gold in his bag, Mr. Hawke said, so Redvers Tremayne has been lucky. Lucky too that no one stole it while he was lying unconscious.

As soon as it was politely possible, I went over to the house, mainly to help. Mr. Tremayne's sisters and mother are usually busy enough as it is with the family and household duties. Dr. Blood had just been as I arrived. When I found Susannah crying in the kitchen I feared the worst but it was simply reaction to the good news Dr. Blood had given. Redvers Tremayne may always walk with a limp but he would survive and no amputations necessary if his legs healed properly. I sat down and cried with her. As she wiped her eyes she regarded me solemnly. She is older than I and perhaps that is why she spoke so directly.

'We never thought Redvers would go to the goldfields, not after he met you, Gweniver. Why do you refuse him?' She hurried on, knowing I would be offended. 'I know you must have because he talks only of you. And it has been two years. And no engagement or anything.' She leaned forward; her whole body spoke the question that her swollen mouth did not. She knew I cared for him too; that there must be a motive for my reticence. Though I could not tell her.

'I thought there was reason enough. Enough reason

that I know would deter most men.'

'Redvers is not "most men", Gweniver.' I almost flinched; how true that was. 'Redvers even follows the concerns of the natives. He's tired of the way they're thought of as less than human, and heathen as though we had brought God with us. He says the Protector of Aborigines should come and sit at one of their campfires by the river before he makes decisions in Adelaide that will affect their lives for generations.'

I smiled. 'He said that?'

She nodded, then leant forward again.

'Gweniver, please consider him. He has said himself he is ashamed of our society, of the way it is in tiers and bound by man-made laws. The Irish are thought little of. We Cornish are looked down upon too. But this is a new country. Gweniver, I'm telling you all this because things can be changed here; Redvers does not think like many other men. He is an accepting man. Sometimes embarrassingly so, but he says he only ever wants to treat others as he'd like to be treated. It is the golden rule, is it not? Whether society thinks it is right or no?'

I sat riveted to my chair. She was describing her brother to a dot. If he could tolerate all these others surely he could accept me. Or would his fine sentiments not stretch that far?

'He lives his faith simply. If it's written in the Bible to love your neighbour, that is what he does. To Redvers, "neighbour" includes everyone.'

I nodded thoughtfully. Mr. Tremayne certainly had the passion to try and change things. Much of the way society was run at home was still in place here. Susannah touched my knee then.

'Please do not underestimate him, Gweniver. We have all known you for more than two years. You are a special person and Redvers is no fool. This talk of honour and respect … what do they mean if they destroy someone's life and happiness? Make a new start, please do. You will make us all very happy.' I sat there staring at her, horror-stricken. It was as if she knew all about me, knew what had happened, what I had done, and it did not matter at all. Could Redvers possibly be the same?

Soon I had the opportunity to find out. Elizabeth took me inside the house to his room and left me there alone. I moved closer to the bed, almost wringing my hands in emotional pain and indecision. I do not deserve this man, one half of me was saying. But you want him, said my heart. *Oh be quiet, heart. Yes, I want him. Then fight. Do not walk away with nothing said.*

'Mr. Tremayne — Redvers?' Suddenly, being polite seemed ludicrous. 'I am truly sorry.' He was regarding me, propped up on two cushions. 'About your accident,' I added. He lifted his hand and I went closer to sit on the chair by his side. His face was scratched and so were his arms. His eyes were dark and shadowed. There were bandages around his shoulders; his legs I could not see.

'M — Gweniver, I missed you.' Speaking seemed difficult, but the little lines at the corners of his mouth started to quiver, as they would when he smiled. And at such moments when one thinks something worse could have happened one's tongue becomes loosened. That is the only way I can explain what I said next. 'And I you.' *Oh God, help me now*, I prayed. Then I went on. 'I am also sorry for refusing you, for I didn't want to.' And I told him about Richard Drew and about what had happened. All of it. The expression on his face barely changed. Perhaps it hurt too much to change it but I could not stand the silence.

'You must be disappointed,' I prodded. Now he would tell me he had met someone else in Bendigo, and would be returning to marry her. A woman who did not refuse his suit, one who had not sinned so badly.

'Gweniver, you never had need to tell me.'

Still in shock, I uttered, 'It is not something I wanted anyone to know.'

'No one will hear it from me.'

But I could not let it rest; I had to know his mind, and his heart. 'Does your offer still stand?' Now that you know everything, I almost added.

'Gweniver, I love you. I loved you more because whatever it was had bothered you so much. It showed you had a pure heart —'

I stood suddenly, knocking the chair. 'You mock me, Sir. You can say that? After what I have told you?'

He almost raised himself off the bed, winced, then thought better of it. 'What happened doesn't change who you are, Gweniver. It is you I love. Not just you with a proviso that you have done nothing wrong. That would be love with conditions. Not true love at all.'

'But everyone says it changes one. To sin in such a way.'

'Are they a greater authority than God?' I shrank at his tone; perhaps it was the pain from the accident (Susannah said his legs were crushed) but I had never heard him quite so passionately angry. 'Where is the charity in this society? Tell me. In Bendigo, I met a young woman who had been transported at twelve years of age for stealing bread for her ailing mother. And where is the charity in forcing a wronged girl to leave her home to find a decent life 10,000 miles away? If we cannot give people second chances, then Christ died for nothing.' He stopped then, calmed himself and apologised; asked to hold my hand in his. 'Gweniver, you are you no matter what happened.'

And suddenly I could see what he was talking about before he went away. The forgiveness. This was the whole reason for going to chapel, for believing in Jesus Christ. The guilt does get taken away. One just has to accept it. Never had I felt forgiven before, nor realised how it worked. It was just as if I was given another opportunity to start living.

What happened may never leave me, but with Redvers loving me, it no longer had power to haunt me. The awful sting of it was gone.

JENEFER

This time I'm taking Kate with me to Mortlock Library and it's not just because Caleb's playing footy. Dad's doing the honours to the railway station and back. Since I'm still on my 'L's, he has to come with me. I must be getting better; he only shouts once.

Aunt Dorie gave me her Cornish teacher's phone number. Get this — the teacher is actually a Bard; I never knew they still had offices like that. She was a wealth of information about Cornwall and its part in the development of South Australia, like the Bible Christians being one of the forerunners of the Uniting Church. So much I never knew. I've already got enough about Gweniver's life here in Kapunda and background material from Kapunda Library for my independent History study. A bit about Cornwall too. Now this is for me. I may never prove Gweniver was also Zenna Dare but I might be able to find more about Gweniver's singing career in Cornwall.

Kate loves Mortlock. Should have brought her before, I guess. The library has organised the inter-library loan and Dad's paid the fifteen dollars for it to come across from Melbourne University. Kate and I take the book into Mortlock, after leaving my student ID with the librarian at the desk. First I get Kate settled onto a computer with the *International Genealogical Index* so she can see how it works. I can almost hear the clackety clack of train wheels as she connects to the web. Then I sit down with my iPad and the book, not so thick fortunately, and find out info that supports what Gweniver wrote on her pages, like who Joseph Emidy was, and all about the Assembly Rooms in Truro. Nothing about Zenna Dare, though. I'm beginning to realise Zenna Dare only sang in London. And then I find a reference to Miss Rundle. I backtrack. It's a quote from an old paper.

> Mr. Drew introduced his new pupil, Miss Rundle, to the Assembly Rooms in Truro this month. She truly is a gem. Not only does she sing well but has a knowledge of Cornwall's musicians and face-to-face has great charm.

It must be Gweniver. The dates fit with the information in her writings. It would have been mid-1846. I keep reading and find only one or two chapters that I need to photocopy. There's only one more reference to Gweniver and this time I'm sure — her whole name is used.

> Gweniver Rundle delighted audiences in Falmouth and Truro, in Tea Gardens, Music Halls and the Assembly Rooms. She sang at balls and concerts in all the major centres during the latter part of 1846. Many young singers began their careers in this way in the early and mid-nineteenth century.

With none of the entertainments we have today, such musical evenings were well attended. Most of the singers, and quite possibly Gweniver Rundle too, would then be introduced to the theatres in London if they were successful in their own counties.

I'm still appalled at the lack of information writers seem to have about individual people in the past, especially ones who weren't terribly famous or at least not for long: 'quite possibly Gweniver Rundle too'. It's so frustrating. A whole book on music in Cornwall in the early nineteenth century and only two references to Gweniver (and nothing concrete) and no reference to Zenna Dare at all. Though that may mean Gweniver didn't have the alias in Cornwall. She, or Richard Drew, must have made it up for London. In case it all went wrong? Then no one would know it was her.

Even then her family may never have heard about it. There was no TV or radio, just newspapers, and what if ordinary miners in Cornwall never saw a London newspaper or magazine? That's presuming they could read. They would never have known. The incident she refers to involving Richard Drew must have happened in London. It's so awesome what I've found out about Gweniver but may never be able to prove. I wonder if I'm the only one who knows.

Kate's finished with the IGI now. She looks all flushed and happy. 'Do you know how many Mary Davies there were in the 1800s?' I shake my head.

'Thousands, Jenfa. Thousands.' Her freckled nose is screwed up and her teeth are showing; she looks cute and she asks me what I found out. Amazing what a bit of attention does for kids. We've decided to buy Steffi some Haigh's chocolates for her birthday. Then I take her to the Blue Lemon, just like Caleb did with me. I push aside the unwelcome image of Amy, Sokha and Ben coming across us that day. When I rang Amy later she was all tight-lipped. It just wasn't the same. Sokha's okay, though. Suppose I shouldn't blame Amy — she's never met an Indigenous person. Nor had I. Wasn't I the same? Sokha says Amy can't work out why I don't go back to the city more. She thinks I've got sunstroke.

'You love Mum, don't you?' Startled, I wonder what I've missed. Kate's talking about Steffi all of a sudden.

'Sure.'

'Then what about your own mum. Was she nice?'

'Dad said she was.'

'You reckon he loves my mum more than yours?'

I stare at her. 'Does it matter now? At the time he loved mine, now he loves yours.' Dad never mentions my mum any more unless I ask. Not since Steffi anyway.

'What happened? She go away?'

'She died.' Why didn't Dad tell the kids all this? Though he wouldn't have known Kate was interested. I didn't until now. It's obvious I haven't said enough. Kate has that 'what next' look on her face.

'We were coming home from the shops. There was an

accident. A car hit ours at an intersection. Mum died.' I find it doesn't really bother me to talk about it — it's just a fact I know — like history. Gweniver seems to affect me more, which is weird.

'Why didn't you?' I check her face; five months ago it would've sounded like she wanted me to have died too, but her features are clear of guile. She just wants to know.

'I was only two. The car seat kept me safe, I guess.'

'That's so sad, Jenfa. I'm glad it didn't happen to me.' I lean closer and hug her. 'If it didn't happen I wouldn't have got you for a sister, now would I?' And that's when Kate tells me.

'Can I tell you something, Jenfa? You won't hate me?'

'I couldn't, could I? You're my sister.' She's regarding me dubiously; she knows that's not a great reason. So do I — look at Gladys and Gweniver — they were sisters. Gladys sure didn't let Gweniver off the hook. My face must have changed, got more serious, for she says it then.

'It was me — I let Sher Khan out. That night —'

Instantly I can remember Hamilton's pitiful sobbing for a tiny rabbit and my own anger at who could be so mean. It's threatening to spill and I'm trying hard not to let it show. This is the old Kate. I thought she'd been better lately. But I relax; she's telling me about then, not now. This is the first time she's come this close so I have to make an effort.

'Why did you do that?'

I expect her to shrug but her eyes fill with tears instead.

'Caleb likes Hamilton better than me.'

'That's not true.'

'It is. He brings things, hay and hutches.'

'Do you really want hay and a hutch?'

She hesitates and I can tell she's thinking Caleb could have easily thought of something different. 'No. But Hamilton's so quiet and everyone thinks he's an angel but he's not. He does things too — stuff Mum and Dad don't see. They see me, that's all.' She sniffs a bit, while I wonder what came first: this behaviour of his or her treatment of him. 'But when he spat the dummy that day — when I locked Sher Khan in the computer room — he was different. He's not a nerdy pushover at all.'

Kate can be surprising, but this is the best bit yet. I'm still trying not to grin at her use of slang that I had no idea she knew.

'You'll need to say sorry, you know. He's still upset.' There's a quick flash of fire in her eyes before she thinks about it. Having little kids for siblings makes me feel so old.

We make our way down to the train and I'm thinking about Zenna Dare again. How weird it is that so much of Gweniver's story is like our own. Kate and I together. And now Kate and Hamilton's too.

GWENIVER

NORTH KAPUNDA, 1852

O, my luve's like a red red rose
  That's newly sprung in June.
O, my luve's like the melodie,
  That's sweetly played in tune.

So fair art thou, my bonnie lass,
  So deep in luve am I:
And I will luve thee still, my dear,
  Till a' the seas gang dry.

Till a' the seas gang dry, my dear,
  And the rocks melt wi' the sun:
And I will luve thee still, my dear,
  While the sands o' life shall run.

And fare thee weel, my only luve,
  And fare thee weel awhile!
And I will come again, my luve,
  Tho' it were ten thousand mile!

Robert Burns 1759–1796

Redvers wants me to marry him before Christmas. He had brought some money back from the goldfields, but he is going to invest it in Nathaniel Hawke's butcher shop so he can build a house later on. Yesterday was the first day he was allowed out of bed by Dr. Blood and he came directly to Mary and Will's to see me and to propose properly. He had his grandmother's ring. But Redvers is apparently a craftsman for he did not just bring a ring. He brought a box. The ring was inside. He made the box before he went to Bendigo; he said he made it for me, because he wanted me to share his home with him. The box is in the shape of a mill cottage with a water wheel just like the ones we have at home. We both know we will never return to Cornwall now. This is our new world and we shall make our life and home in it together.

It nearly made me weep when I saw him limp to the front door, helped by his new young friend, Nathaniel, who carried the box. What I had nearly missed through my terrible burden of guilt. And now I hardly feel it at all. There is only Redvers' love and acceptance. It is Redvers who has shown me what love can be, what even God's love is. Now I understand how Mary Magdalene must have felt.

Mary showed them into the parlour, but Nathaniel quickly smiled and left. Redvers was still pale, and there were lines in his face that showed coming at all was a painful effort. I rushed forward with a chair.

'Please, sit down.' Mary went to make tea happily with a wink at me and one hand pulling a protesting Annie out of the room. Truly I feel I have never been so happy. Only one thing could make me even happier and that is impossible of course.

Redvers had difficulty kneeling due to his injury so he

asked me to stand beside him so he could look up into my face. First he asked me to open the box. I could not as it had a secret opening, but he gave me clues, and then I found the ring. He took my hand and called me his white lily. I could tell he was challenging me to contradict him but I did not dare. I had learnt my lesson.

We sat together then, our hands linked. His kiss was just as sweet as I thought it would be.

JENEFER

From: Rossworld
To: Jenefer Tremayne
Subject: Zenna Dare

Dear Jenefer

Don't know if you have seen this but I came across it in my travels through cyber space — an obscure US uni site on English theatre history. Have just forwarded the URL to you. Hope it is still useful.

Regards

Ross

> Miss Zenna Dare treated London to three glorious talent-filled seasons, and then suddenly disappeared from public view, never to perform again. Gossipmongers of the time spoke of a fallout with her manager or worse, of moral shame, but anyone who saw the virginal Zenna Dare would know this to be untrue. The sad fact is she may have died or retired quietly, or even emigrated to America or the colonies. If the latter is true, she never resumed her singing career. We would have heard if she took New York or Sydney by storm, as indeed she would have, if she had stayed under Sir Richard Drew's management.

So Richard Drew got knighted. For his contribution in finding musical talent, no doubt. I'm in my room again, just wondering about everything. Should be doing homework of course. Mr Mayes has said I could rewrite the last few chapters of *Tess of the d'Urbervilles* for my end-of-semester English assignment. But it was my own triple-great-grandfather who rewrote *Tess of the d'Urbervilles*. If there were more people like Redvers we wouldn't have had so many Stolen Children (or people staring at Caleb and me on trains). If only Angel Clare were like Redvers. But then Angel Clare wasn't a 'howling Methodist'. What dreadful labels people put on others. So incredible how ignorant I was. Even about Caleb. And I don't care anymore if some of the kids at school have reservations about it — that's their problem. At least Steffi thinks Caleb is great. It would make a good tourist ad: Come to Kapunda — have your life changed forever.

Now the box is left in the special place in the window space. It's left open often and Kate comes when she likes to read my typed-up pages to get ideas for illustrations. I tell her that when we're older we'll make a good team; she can illustrate my books. Just at study time I can never resist looking in the house, trying to find a clue that I've missed. In the letter case there are only the pages left that were ripped up. They were even screwed up before that. And now they are here. Gweniver wasn't very sure about what to do. I just have to piece them together. I turn the wheel, insert the key — every time I do this I get an incredible feeling of Gweniver having done it before. Her feelings fill the room sometimes and I know it's only my fancy, as

Steffi calls it, or because I'm reading Gweniver's story, but it's there all the same.

Knowing someone's story sure is powerful stuff. It brings so much understanding and empathy. I sense there's still more I need to do. Did she want us to know she was a singer, was that it? Or was it something to do with the family? It won't hurt if I get the little pieces out of the case and try and put them together. Ready for later.

I'm just getting the last piece out, when my jumper catches on a little wood partition next to the ink bottle. I tug and suddenly there's a clunk. Incredible! Under the inkwell and place for the pen, there's a drawer! Maybe to someone in the nineteenth century a drawer under the inkwell wouldn't be a surprise but it sure is to me. In it is a folded flat paper. Another one. I unfold it. It's got a line right through it, had been scrunched up as well, with a poem on the back. It's the letter she never sent — she must have put it here and forgotten about it.

GWENIVER

Dear Gladys

I hope this letter finds everyone well at home. I am writing to let you know I have arrived safely. The voyage was too hideous to describe to you here. Suffice it to say only nine died, nor did we capsize at Cape Horn as Mama feared.

Mary and Will are well as are little Emily and George. Mary is expecting a third and may be delivered by Easter. They are making their way in this new land with courage and forbearance. It is so unlike Cornwall that I do not know where to start to describe it. I could not have imagined the far side of the moon to be as different as this place is. The heat, the flies, the mosquitoes, the ants. Wherever one puts a foot one needs eyes on it to check for vermin. The black people seemed frightening at first, but are amiable enough. I wonder what they think about us all here, sharing this land. They are so at home in it and yet we try to tame it into something we can understand.

How I wish our society was different and I could still have Roswyn with me. But I know she will have a good life at home. My arms ache at times and I console myself with

Mary's little Emily. An exile I am, but I understand it is my own doing. My punishment could not be worse.

The Secret Rose

My secret rose, it is too soon,
Yet not before I see
The blueness of your wondering eyes
As they look up at me.
My tiny Roswyn, all too soon
They snatched you from my arms;
But not before your little hand
Lay warm between my palms.
O Roswyn, little tender rose,
Your mother do not blame;
Just two things could I give to you:
Your life and then your name.

G.R

JENEFER

There was a child! No wonder Gweniver was always so sad. I should have guessed. Steffi would have, I bet. Gweniver had to give up her child and leave her in Cornwall. Where, I wonder? With the family?

This can't wait. It's the middle of the night but I log onto the 'net. I have to find out for sure that Roswyn was her child. I enter in *International Genealogical Index* on the web. When it appears I type a name: Roswyn Rundle. No hits. Roswyn Drew? No hits again. Roswyn by itself: there are too many — screens of them. I have to narrow it down. Who did Mary say in her letter Gladys had married? I run across to my room and check. It's a long shot but who would you leave a child with if you couldn't take her to the Colonies? With a sister, surely. And Gweniver wrote to Gladys; it must have been Gladys. If she left Roswyn with Clarice I'm in trouble; I don't know who Clarice married, or even if she did.

I try again: Roswyn Penwith. And there she is. Not a birth, but a christening.

Roswyn Rundle, daughter of James Penwith and Gladys Rundle, christened Camborne Wesleyan Chapel, 14th August 1849.

I stare at the screen. Is this proof? What if Gladys had a daughter called Roswyn and Gweniver just liked her? But would they give Roswyn a second name of Rundle if she wasn't Gweniver's? But why would Gweniver call her 'my little rose', and say 'snatched from my arms'? No, she must have been Gweniver's. And she was being christened while Gweniver was on the ship to South Australia! I scroll down the screen. Lots of kids have second names and yes, some are the mother's maiden name. Gladys was a Rundle too. Roswyn's adoption was carefully covered up. I bet illegitimate births weren't registered often because of the shame of it in those days. Is that why there is no entry for Roswyn's birth? I sit there for a while, soaking it all in. *Poor Gweniver, what you must have gone through.* Who took her in? Her friend, the old organ grinder? Was he the only one who understood?

And suddenly I know what I have to do.

There's no point sleeping now. I click onto marriages in the IGI. Just hope Dad won't get too hyper if I overstep the monthly Internet allowance. We should have free Internet access like they do in the States.

```
INTERNATIONAL GENEALOGICAL INDEX
Country: Cornwall
Name: Roswyn Penwith
Birth death or Marriage: marriage
Dates: 1860–1888
Result of your search:
Roswyn Rundle Penwith m Nicholas Hayes
Camborne Parish, Corn, 17th March 1868
```

Yes. Now a surname search. There are all these links. When you finally understand what you want to know, it's almost like the web stretches out sticky strands and draws you in. Soon I'm whizzing along a highway in the genealogy web ring, and I couldn't stop if I wanted to.

```
GLOBAL SURNAME SEARCH
RootsWeb
Country: Cornwall
Surname: Hayes
Your name: Tremayne, Jenefer Joy
Names you are searching for:
Hayes, Rundle, Penwith
Your message:
I am looking for a Roswyn Rundle
Penwith who married Nicholas Hayes
in 1868 in Camborne, Cornwall
```

I hope someone on this chat line is researching Hayes or Rundle. I had never realised how many people are excited by this stuff. That there could be people out there researching my family; people who could be writing me into their family tree and I'd be oblivious to it all.

GWENIVER

Now cease, my lute: this is the last
Labour that thou and I shall waste,
And ended is that we begun;
Now is this song both sung and past:
My lute be still, for I have done.

Sir Thomas Wyatt 1503–1542

How will I survive this? I must end it. No girl lives through such a catastrophe without shame to herself and to her family. When I go home, I shall throw myself from the cliffs at Portreath. Even that is wicked, but I do not deserve any better. I will always be a burden on my family. And Richard. In his cards and letters he's trying to make it seem he cares. But I know him. He will never marry me. So I will not give myself the extra pain of hearing him sidestep his responsibility. Never will I tell him what has happened. How I could ever have compromised myself in this way I will never know. Mama will say, 'You! How could 'ee!' Da will be disgusted. I cannot bear to imagine Gladys's recriminations.

Was it only a dream? He said I was a songbird. What hopes I had, what fire in my belly for all those things he said I could achieve. It is all gone now. Richard calls me by another name but it is not me he loves, it is her, the girl he has created. She is the one who wears what he decides, sings what he wants, and even eats his favourite dishes. I can never live up to what he expects. 'Tis only Gweniver Rundle I am, a simple Cornish girl. A fool I was to think I could be any different.

Recently I could tell Richard's affections had changed. He was more attentive, in a way I did not understand. It was not like a proper courtship. Courtship and marriage I understand, not that predatory stalking of me. How long has it gone on? These three years? Was he waiting until I was old enough? Or was he gradually wearing me down? But I never was a party to it. He can have my deflowering on his conscience forever. Yet it must have been my fault. If I did not go to Penzance, if I did not go on tour. Perhaps that was the turning point, he must have thought I felt the same. Oh God, I sold my soul.

When it finally happened, I left. I will not live as his kept woman. This is hell enough. He will not meet with me again for I shall never answer his cards.

JENEFER

In just two days I've received six e-mails. Incredible. Two from the States. One of those says they are descendants from a Thomas Rundle from Camborne who emigrated to California. Even though it's quite possibly Gweniver's brother, Tommy, I can't get sidetracked. I send a polite answer back saying who I am. If I don't stay on Roswyn's trail I could end up anywhere. This feels like a rabbit warren with too many turns and no radar to find my way. Most of the messages were from the UK but were not of our family. That I know of anyway. But there's one e-mail from Canberra and this is the one that gets me writing a feverish reply.

Dear Jenefer
What a lovely Cornish name you have and spelt correctly too. I'm not of the Hayes family you are after but I've been doing some Hayes global surname research and I know of someone who is researching your side of the family: Joan and Bill Hayes. They will be very happy to hear from you. Just click on the address below. Keep me posted — I'd love to hear how it all goes.
Regards
John Hayes

Dear Joan and Bill
I am a descendant of Gweniver Rundle who emigrated

to South Australia in 1849. Gweniver was sister to Gladys Penwith who brought up Roswyn, christened 1849. Are you from this family? Please contact me if you are.
Regards
Jenefer Tremayne

Dear Jenefer
This is amazing! How exciting! We are in Cornwall and have been trying to trace our Australian connection for years. We knew of a Mary who went to Kapunda. Then a Gweniver who left for South Australia too, but no one's ever known if she survived the trip out. Not much was ever said of her — a black sheep most probably. Gladys was an old tyrant and wouldn't allow her to be spoken of — some rift in the family. Seems a pity to me. Even Mary lost contact. Are you a direct descendant? Tell us all about yourself. Bill can't even sit down he's that excited.
We are in our forties and have two children: Nick, twenty, and Tammy, eighteen. They're both in university. You mentioned only Roswyn. We wondered why. There were many other brothers and sisters. Roswyn was the second eldest and was my husband's great-grandmother.
Write soon. Tonight.
Warm wishes
Joan and Bill

Dear Joan and Bill
I am almost seventeen and in Year 12 here. I live in Kapunda, South Australia, where Gweniver came to be with her sister Mary. Do you know anything more about Roswyn? Or a Zenna Dare?
Regards
Jenefer

Dear Jenefer

This is Tam. Isn't this fantastic? I had no idea we had cousins in Australia. How big is Kapunda? Is it a village? Or a suburb of Adelaide? Mum said to tell you we have a photo of a Zenna Dare, though no one knows who she was. It was with some things of great-great-grandma Roswyn Hayes. We'll get Nick to scan it and send it if you like.

Tell us some more. What secrets have you uncovered? I'd like to know why Gweniver left here single. Not many did unless they were orphans.

Cheers
Tam

Dear Tam

I desperately would like a copy of the photo. I think Gweniver was a singer and her stage name was Zenna Dare. I have no proof though. It's just that we have a photo of her too, and I'm desperate for any clue. Though your photo may only be the same as ours. Kapunda has about 4000 people — it's a country town. Is that the same as a village? I live in the house Gweniver lived in a few years after she married Redvers Tremayne. I think it's cool too — having cousins in Cornwall. I had no idea. Six months ago I didn't even know where I came from. So awesome.

Bye
Jenefer

Just pressed the send button. I can't bring myself to tell them Gweniver's secret; not about Roswyn. They all believe Gladys is their triple-great-grandmother. How can I change all that now? Roswyn must never have been told. Or it would be written in a family Bible or something.

They'd know surely. What exactly did Gweniver want the box to do? Maybe it's too late now.

Caleb hasn't come to the Year 12 room to go home yet so I decide to find him. The Ag Science area is first port of call. Although there are some Year 10s there, swishing out their cattle yards, Caleb is nowhere. No one's seen him. Then I think of the art room. Of course. If Caleb's not playing footy, or in the Ag Science area, he's finishing off art work. His subjects sure take up heaps of time; hardly ever see him at lunch any more. I spend most of my lunches with Erin and even then it's watching her practising for the Year 12 drama. So glad I don't do drama. Erin does music as well and she has to sing in the play — it's a send-up of *Pirates of Penzance*; it's called *Psychedelic Shores*. Erin plays Mabel and has to dance on a surf board to Dirty Dancing music. We saw a video of the original — it had Gary Allen in it as the Pirate King. Chris Haynes is the only guy doing drama, and has to be Frederick. (There's no Pirate King — too bad.) Chris doesn't sing as well as Erin. I reckon Caleb would do a better job, but of course I don't tell anyone.

Caleb has to finish his painting early, before assessment, so it can be hung in the hall for the drama night. All the kids doing any sort of art subjects are feverishly working for this display. Some are doing sculpture. Tim and another friend are putting together an animated cartoon on computer. Each frame was sculpted from plasticine before it was photographed. Incredible.

When I reach the art room, it's quiet. No one there. Just about to leave when I see it standing against the wall. It has to be Caleb's painting. Huge. Six foot wide at least and all done in the earth colours he loves so much: red, yellow, white, brown and black. I can see the land, sweeping from one corner to the other, a dam, trees — his peppermint gums? Dots that look like raindrops; they're not perfectly round. I look closer; just above the little black and white feet walking across the canvas, there are hands, and under the hands, incredible — it's music, little dots with tails that seem alive, swirling across the red, and up into the clouds. I'm standing here just staring; everywhere I look there's something more to see.

There's a movement behind me. Caleb. 'Found the painting, eh? Like it?' He sounds shy and I turn quickly. 'Yeah, I like it.' How can I say how incredible it is — it's about everything he cares about — nature: the land, animals, camels, yes, even a tiny rabbit. And then he tells its story. He does it respectfully like it's a painting he's found in a cave from 20,000 years ago.

'These white lines? They're ripples of water. The clouds are where God is, the Spirit of the Land — he overlooks everything regardless of how it turns out. The raindrops are the tears when children were taken away.' I look carefully, most are black, a few are white. I think of Gweniver. 'These are the ones who got lost, who didn't make it.' He points to a crowd of shapes that look like dots with wings and I guess he's thinking of his uncle. How many others were there? The hands. 'The hands are so important — we do everything with them, work together, learn. They show how we care for things, like the land, our culture. And the feet — we can all walk together too.'

'The music?'

'And the music.' He doesn't explain, just looks like he's seeing it for the first time too, and I realise the painting is everyone's story. The story of his family and culture, of the land that's so important to who he is, but a bigger story too. The clasped hands at the bottom, one white, one black — his and mine? But not just ours. No wonder the art teacher wants it in the hall. If this painting had sound, it would be a symphony, its grand harmonies inviting all to listen to the truth within their hearts.

When I get home I tell myself I really should finish some work for school. Semester's nearly over, but I just check the e-mail first. Won't take long.

Dear Jenefer
Nick's away on camp but he'll send the photo as soon as he gets back. I'm not sure about the different type of file to send so that you'll see it okay. You still should get it before snail mail anyway. I forgot to tell you. I was talking to my Grandad this morning. He's so adorable and as sharp as old cheese. Get this. He

remembers Roswyn! Thought you might like that since you mentioned her. Roswyn was his grandma, she died in 1925, he said, when she was in her late seventies. He was fifteen and remembers her clearly.
Cheers
Tam

Dear Tam
Please ask your Grandad to write to me, or could you ask him to send an e-mail. Does he know how to do that?
Please, Tam. Most of my really old olds have died. I've got a great-aunt, but nothing like a Grandad who is as old as yours. You should be so lucky.
Love Jenefer

Dear Jenefer
I've got Grandad here and he's going to talk while I type. (He comes over every day — has to keep walking to keep his circulation going.) Here goes:
My dear Jenefer
This is a very big thrill for me to be meeting you like this. Tamara is typing — don't think I could see the keys properly now. You asked about my Grandmother Roswyn.
She was the mildest lady. We all loved her. Always gave me a penny when I went to see her when I was little. Grandpa was dead by then. Grandma always loved music. She had a Master's Voice gramophone and on Saturday nights a lot of our family would go there and she would put on a record. No one was allowed to touch it, though. She had a most beautiful singing voice, even then, and she sometimes would sing along. Her mother (Gladys) was a tough old lady — she would never let Roswyn have singing lessons or do anything with her talent. She believed the stage only produced

fallen women. So when Grandma Roswyn married, she let my mother and aunts all have singing lessons. Some of them did quite well too. And music has been a part of our family ever since. Even I can still play the violin on a good day. Grandma paid for the lessons and made sure we had a piano in the house. The other aunts used to wonder where all the talent came from. Hope this is interesting to you.
Best regards
Pawley Hayes
Cheers from Tam (your fifth cousin) too.
PS Isn't Grandad brilliant?

Tam thinks she's my fifth cousin, but they don't know about Roswyn; we're most probably fourth cousins. Straight away I send a reply to Pawley.

Dear Mr Hayes
I guess you must be like a second cousin to me. Thank you so much for telling me about your grandma. I found her name mentioned in something of Gweniver's. No doubt Roswyn would have been born just before Gweniver left for South Australia; she must have been fond of the baby.
Many thanks, Jenefer

Oh Pawley, I know why you could play the violin so well. Richard Drew was a virtuoso if the reviews can be believed. Pawley's my second cousin, twice removed. Worked that out from a family relationship table on the web. Incredible, eh? I wish I could tell him, but I don't dare — not until I'm sure it wouldn't upset him. Wish I could meet him.

Dear John

Thank you so much for putting me onto the Hayes family in Cornwall.

It turns out we're related and they were looking for us! It's incredible finding the other half of your family, especially when you didn't know it existed.

Thanks again

Bye, Jenefer

I've finally managed to tape up the second ripped page. It was easier than I thought since the writing is different, smaller and more ordered than Gweniver's scrawl. The first one was something Gweniver had written before she left Cornwall. And if Gweniver's name were only on this one, it'd prove my theory about Zenna Dare. Wonder why she never burnt it or threw it out? Did people go through the rubbish in those days? Was keeping it the only way to make it stay a secret? Or did she keep it as a memory of the dream she had. Poor Gweniver. I wonder how you let go of a dream?

Dear Zenna

Where are you? Why do you not answer my messages? See,
I have copied this poem from a Shelley anthology and write
your name within.

To Zenna
The keen stars were twinkling,
And the fair moon was rising among them,
Dear Zenna!
The guitar was tinkling,
But the notes were not sweet till you sang them
Again.
As the moon's soft splendour
O'er the faint cold starlight of Heaven
Is thrown,
So your voice most tender
To the strings without soul had then given
Its own.
The stars will awaken,
Though the moon sleep a full hour later,
To-night;
No leaf will be shaken
Whilst the dews of your melody scatter
Delight.
Though the sound overpowers,
Sing again, with your dear voice revealing
A tone
Of some world far from ours,
Where music and moonlight and feeling
Are one.

Please tell me where you are. You have disappeared as surely
and mysteriously as your famous namesake at Zennor. Do not
let it end like this. Please. R.

JENEFER

It's nearly teatime; Kate's drawing in the lounge and Hamilton's picking out tunes on the piano. Steffi's putting a little table that she's just waxed in the kitchen to dry and Dad's cooking his favourite pasta: pesto with pine nuts, with *Phantom of the Opera* blaring so loud on the sound system I can hear it down here. Dad's been getting into music ever since he saw the box. Kate's Celtic storybook tells me all about the Merrymaid of Zennor, how she was Cornwall's most famous mermaid and had an exquisite voice. In human form she fell in love with the church warden's son and they both disappeared. Richard Drew must have thought of Gweniver's alias after he'd taken her to Lamorna Cove and showed her that rock. Everything is falling into place, in my mind at least, even though I have no conclusive proof.

Now I've just got time to check the e-mail. E-mail has never been so addictive. Can't stop thinking about Roswyn; she must have been Gweniver's child. The Hayes don't know about it, but Roswyn's musical talent, the fact there is no birth date recorded, the musical talent in the family — it all fits.

Dear Jenefer

Grandad's still talking about you. He can't get over it. Nick's home at last. We're sending the photo you wanted and one of us too, plus the family tree Dad's been drawing up for the past ten years! Nick says he hopes jpeg files will be okay on your system. Let us know if there is a problem. Tell us too if Zenna Dare is who you think. It all sounds so fantastical, though Dad's not surprised — says musical talent does run through our side of the family. Even Nick plays the sax when he feels like it. He's good too.

Cheers Tam

PS We've included another photo that looks like the same lady. And Gweniver's will. We still have the lute that looks like the one in the photo — hugely old. Grandad says it was Roswyn's. Cheers.

PPS Let's be friends on Facebook.

I try not to get too excited by the mention of the lute as I stare at the icons shouting *attachment.* They squat on the screen, insignificant squares, out-staring me, unblinking, daring me to double click on them. This may be nothing at all. Like Roswyn, Gweniver may keep Zenna's secret until eternity. I click on one. It's the family tree. I print it out to study later. Roswyn is shown as Gladys's second child. The next one is the picture of Tam's family. They look nice. Bill is dark, so is Nick. Tam looks like her mum.

I click on the next attachment; watch the little dotted lines flicker and materialise into a black and white photograph. The lute! It's Gweniver— it has to be. Looks like her. Hard to tell sometimes, with these old photos. No name, though. She's in a gypsy costume. For *The Bohemian*

Girl? It's possible Richard Drew had it done. Maybe that was how the daguerreotype photos came about when Aunt Dorie said the family could never have afforded it. They were Richard Drew's. For publicity? Or did he have a soft spot for Gweniver, even in the beginning? For all I know Gweniver misjudged Richard Drew completely. There was never any publicity about Zenna Dare after 1848, so he may have kept her identity secret — maybe he did care after all. But I'm not sorry now she came to South Australia. If she didn't I would never have been born.

I still can't call the lute proof. Someone could say the photo just looks like Gweniver, or what does dressing up as a gypsy prove — so what? The will comes up next. Nick's scanned it in. And there on my computer screen is Gweniver's squirly writing. Suddenly, more than anything this links me with the Hayes family across the world in Cornwall, more than any of their words have done, even more than Pawley contacting me.

WRITTEN ON THIS 30TH DAY OF JULY 1849:

I, Gweniver Rundle, of Fore Street, Camborne, of sound mind and before God, state that if I should not reach the colony of South Australia, I do bequeath all my worldly goods to my sister Gladys to distribute as she should see fit. My lute and other goods of value that I cannot take, I hereby leave in Gladys's care.

As God is my witness, Gweniver Rundle.

Guess the Hayes family wouldn't know why everything was left to Gladys, and who it would be distributed to. I click on the next attachment. I'm not really expecting anything; I'm getting used to the idea of never knowing for sure. The photo materialises on the screen.

For a full second I stare at it. It couldn't be for more than that one moment, just long enough for the phantom to call for his angel of music and then I stand up; the chair clatters on the slate and I yelp. It's meant to be a scream but it freezes on the way out.

'What!' Kate comes thumping down the stairs. The piano stops abruptly and Hamilton's steps follow her. 'Jenfa! What have you done?' Kate's in here now and she sees the screen; slowly walks up to it. All she can say is 'Jenfa' with an un-Kate-like awe.

I nod. My chest is starting to heave — I can't help it. The shock of not expecting to find out and then — this!

'It's the dress.' She looks back at me, to check. 'Isn't it?'

'Yeah.' I breathe it out like a quiet sob. And I stare again at the beautiful lace right up to her neck. She sure does look virginal — the reviews were right. Underneath is written: *Miss Zenna Dare*. She's smiling at someone to the right of the camera. She looks like she's just sung the most beautiful aria ever and the audience has asked for five encores. Zenna is an elusive phantom no longer — she was real and she was Gweniver.

Kate runs into my room across the hall; she's only gone a minute and brings in the white dress from the box,

Gweniver's dress. 'Careful' I say. I've never dared unfold it — it's so old — and here's Kate carrying it in. The skirt slips out of her arms, uncurls, and I stop at how lovely it is. It too has exquisite lace right up to the neck. A waist Dad could put two hands around, the V in the front bodice cascading lace to the floor. She wasn't so tall. None of us see the paper that falls from its folds.

Oh Gweniver, now we know. Then I say this next bit really slow. 'Kids, our great-great-great grandmother was a famous opera singer.' Kate starts squealing so that Steffi and Dad come rushing down.

'We know now!' Kate's jumping, and Hamilton's laughing. Check that. Yep, Hamilton's laughing.

But I don't tell them about Roswyn. Not yet. Maybe never. Maybe some things are meant to be secret. What if I was the only one meant to know.

It's not until much later that I decipher the paper Steffi has picked up from the floor.

GWENIVER

South Kapunda 1858

Long my imprisoned spirit lay
*   Fast bound in sin and nature's night;*
Thine eye diffused a quickening ray —
*   I woke, the dungeon flamed with light;*
My chains fell off, my heart was free,
I rose, went forth, and followed Thee.

Charles Wesley 1707–88

How I loved to sing those hymns when young and loved them for their tunes, their beauty of phrase, not understanding the truth hidden therein. Redvers is correct — our society is hardly Christian at all. Everyone believes it is, but what Christ taught rises far above our puny rules of what to wear and how to act. He taught a love of God and of each other; if we could only embrace that sentiment we would not be forcing others to be like ourselves.

Not everyone agrees with Redvers, I have noticed, especially when he starts discussing Native Affairs. The Irish too. He thinks better cottages should be built for the miners and if money was spread around a bit more there would be enough for everyone. Even Mr. Richard Hawke, who treats Redvers like a nephew, was cautioning him after chapel last week. He has said before that Redvers' lack of ecclesiastical training enables him to see things in a fresh light. But this time he told him to bide his time a little more.

Redvers told me afterwards that too much time gets abided and not enough done to help those in need. I think he wishes he were one of the gentlemen with the money and he would put it to better use. At least he has built this lovely house. There is plenty of room, even more allowed for in case it is needed: a room under the stairs that could be furnished. I have started a garden and yesterday Redvers helped me plant a pepper tree by the front gate, and the little white roses are flourishing by the verandah. Everyone says gardens will not grow here for the fumes from the mine, but we will prove them wrong.

The items I brought with me to this country I have packaged up. The dress I had to bring with me, regardless of the room in the trunk. It was one I wore in happier times. There are the things I wrote before I married Redvers too. What soul searching I went through, writing it all down, hoping to find some peace of mind. And Redvers has always been true to his promise; he has always treated me with the utmost love and respect and has never referred to my old life unless I myself brought it up. Redvers approves of the idea of putting my past to rest, entombing it as it were, in the cottage box. At first I was going to burn the things, but I still hold a hope that some day when it does not matter so much, something can be done.

The family was so divided and I caused it all. Gladys only consented to have Roswyn if I never contacted them. She said it would be best for the child. Now I wish for everyone to be reconciled and be a whole family again. Gladys was even cross with Mary for offering me a home in South Australia. What did Gladys expect me to do? Live in the poor-house? I did not deserve Mary's kindness but she was always like that. She saw beyond the hypocrisy of the rules that have been made. Just like dear Redvers.

Perhaps with this box left here, Roswyn can be written to and told how much I love her, that it was either South Australia or death for me, or shame for us both; that in the society we were part of, there was no alternative.

If this box should ever be found I pray it will only be seen as the out-pouring of a mother's heart. I have suffered the loss of Roswyn all my life and will continue to do so. Every birthday I think, 'Roswyn will be such-and-such-an-age today. I wonder if she's alive, if she is well, what she is doing.'

For me it can never be the end. Can a mother's heart ever forget?

The White Rose

I love the white rose in its splendour,
I love the white rose in its bloom.
I love the white rose, so fair as she grows
It's the rose that reminds me of you.
The first time I met you, my darling,
Your face was as red as a rose;
But now your dear face has grown paler,
As pale as the lily-white rose.
And now that you've left me forever,
From your grave one sweet flower grows,
But I will remember you, darling,
When I gaze on that lily-white rose.

JENEFER

My instincts were right. Gweniver wrote only Roswyn should know and for the family rift to be mended. Well, Roswyn's dead but the rift's been healed — it's enough. It's what Gweniver wanted. She just didn't know it would take 160 years. It would be easy to tell, to feel everyone's admiration for being able to find out. Caleb's been taught that reconciliation doesn't happen until the stories are told and understood, but surely there are some things that only a few know? Nor can I bring myself to tell this part yet. Gweniver's grief and fear were real and they feel too close, even now; it would be flippant to blurt it all out as if she hadn't suffered at all. Yet I think Caleb would be proud of me all the same. I hope Gweniver is too.

Can't believe Dad and I walked down to church early this morning. This is how it happened. Last night I had a go at him about religion. Gweniver practically said they would never have survived without this faith of theirs. What happened to all that? Was it all just fairy stories like the knockers and mermaids? So I asked Dad. 'Why don't you and I believe something, like Steffi?' And Great-aunt Dorie; she still calls herself a Methodist. Poor Dad. You should have seen him; it was like he was the victim of a hit-and-run truck driver. Guess it was one question he never thought I'd ask.

'I thought you could make up your own mind when you got older.' Well now I'm older and I have no idea and I told him so.

'Isn't it your job to offer the option so I can accept or reject it?'

Dad started scratching his stubble and I knew I'd see the inside of the Uniting Church this morning. I didn't see anyone from school nor a miracle or golden lights but I did get to see lots of Tremaynes on the Honour Roll: the famous Albert who went to the Boer War and World War One yet managed to return, and a Dickie who died in World War Two. And we sang the same Wesleyan hymn that Gweniver wrote on her last page. Nothing much has changed but that may not be bad either.

Now it's Steffi's birthday lunch. She's also decided to celebrate the opening of her shed out the back. She's got a sign over the top: *Restored First-Loves*. Dad's been to get Aunt Dorie and in she comes laden with a huge basket, and smelling of purple hair rinse and spray. Caleb's here too in his best jeans. I catch a look in Aunt Dorie's eyes as she first sees Caleb. It reminds me of Amy and I stiffen; I've learnt these past few months that people's disapproval affects me more than I used to think, but happily Aunt Dorie is more polite than Amy. The look fades as she sees him playing with the kids. This time he brought something for Kate. She must have shown him her drawings of the mine and the house for he pulls out these special art crayons. Kate's practically steaming over with creative energy as he shows her how to use them. Hamilton shows Caleb the screeds of stuff Kate has found for him on the 'net about rabbits. 'Cool. I could do my Ag Science final study with all this research.' He grins over at me; guess he's teasing me again. It's fun watching him sprawled on the floor, the two kids practically on top of him, making sure they get their share of his attention.

Aunt Dorie is calling to me from the couch to come and sit with her. Now she has this look in her eyes that I can't quite read. Dad must have told her about Zenna Dare (maybe about church too) for she looks kind of impressed, but there's a shrewd type of reserve there too. And it makes me wonder what she thinks about it all. The family Bible comes out of the basket first.

'Emily finally remembered.' There's no apology that I asked for it months ago. And suddenly I'm looking at Gweniver's squirly penmanship again. The names of the children that I now know. Baby Rebekah who died. Marriages. There are more photos. The wedding photo. Without fully smiling, Redvers managed to look like the cat that got the cream, and Gweniver — she's older but there's the likeness to that beautiful girl who once sang for a queen.

Aunt Dorie shows me another: two boys staring

solemnly at the camera, violins under their chins, bows poised. Wonder what happened to those violins. I voice this aloud.

'Their descendants have them, I suppose,' Aunt Dorie answers. And I think about the lady in the antique shop; how she made it sound as though we had so many rellies. We most probably do. Think about eight kids having children down five generations. There could be over a thousand of us walking around Adelaide with different names, brushing against each other down Rundle Mall and never knowing we were related. Aunt Dorie wants to see the pages I've typed up. Ms East calls them transcriptions. Cool word, eh? I show the folder I'm putting together for History with the illustrations Kate has finished already. Aunt Dorie reads through the one I wrote myself for the introduction — how I thought Gweniver must have felt as Zenna Dare, singing for a queen at Drury Lane. She reads a few of the transcripts, sniffs and tells me I've done a lot of good work. Then she hands me this old notebook.

'I think you'll find this interesting, Jenefer. Emily had it.'

The book is cloth-bound, sewn, with blank pages. As soon as I open it I can tell it's the very book Gweniver used to write in, for most of the pages have been torn out. There's an entry near the back.

17TH MARCH 1868

R would be nineteen today. I pray she is well and happy. Redvers found a snake under the twins' bed; all sorts of vermin seem to find their way down here. So he is closing off the room the children play in. We have not used it for much else; the older children all sleep together across the hall and the little ones with us. Besides, the room is so cold, and we have a cellar already. No one will find the cottage box now I suppose, although Redvers says if something is meant to be it will be, when the time is right.

Aunt Dorie is looking at the page. She would have read it. How much does she know? Does she suspect anything about the box? About Roswyn?

'I'm not sure what she was referring to, Jenefer.' There's almost a question in her voice but not quite. She's not as anxious to know as I was. 'Perhaps R was the little one who died.'

I nod, even though I can't imagine that Aunt Dorie isn't able to add or subtract. Rebekah would only have been eight in 1868. I glance up suddenly and find Aunt Dorie regarding me steadily. Great-aunt Dorie. She's a widow and childless. She looks just like a sexless old maid, someone who doesn't have a life. Will some sixteen-year-old look at me when I'm eighty and think I've had no life? But Aunt Dorie's eyes are not lifeless; they still have that calculating look in them. And it strikes me it's not improbable that she's caught on after all. It's possible she had suspicions even before I went to see her earlier in the year. I'll never find out, of course; if she knows she would never tell.

In light of this I think it won't hurt to ask her what the name Roswyn would mean in Cornish. I do and there's a trace of a smile on those old lipsticked pink lips of hers as she says, 'White rose, I should think, dear.' I try and keep the smirk of satisfaction off my face.

Then Steffi's calling us to the table and it turns out to be a fun time with Dad showing off as usual; telling pitiful jokes. It's nice to see Steffi happy; she and Dad holding hands every now and then. Sher Khan only disgraces himself once, as he leaps from Hamilton's lap across Aunt Dorie's to the hallway door. Afterwards, when everyone settles down in the lounge with the wood fire blazing, Caleb and I escape for a walk.

'You have a nice family,' is Caleb's first comment. I'm impressed because I reckon he'd know. Imagine if I'd never met him, never found out what I know about his family.

I must have seemed so snobby that first day at school, trying not to show how scared I was. Though Erin told me recently that she knew I wasn't a snob or I wouldn't have spoken to Caleb. That had made me think for a while, especially about school and Kapunda. Ashleigh and I get on okay — we have something in common, of course: we're relatively new — and Erin's loosened up a lot. Maybe she's got used to seeing Caleb as someone more than just Tim's mate. Guess I'll never know what was bothering her, for I've realised it's not something she could talk about since Tim is Caleb's best friend and what if I told Caleb?

It still seems to take forever to get used to a new place, even if it is friendly and your ancestors were here. And how long does it take to be accepted? I still don't know. And next year I'll have to go to uni — will that be a daily train trip or boarding with Auntie Joy? Wonder if Caleb and I will still see each other and if he'll visit me in the city. Will I even want to come back? So much to think about and we haven't even finished first semester yet; there's still the drama night, and mock exams to study for. Caleb reckons I should give myself a break. Just like he said, I can't do anything about Chloe — she has to work it out herself. He reckons Kapunda is the same. So what if it takes ages, he said. You be happy where you are in the meantime. He said it like it was a choice I could make and that it was seriously important.

We're walking down to the mine. I still find it weird to think that the place where my triple-great-grandfather first worked is now a tourist trail. There are all these wide pools full of green water. That's the copper. And dangerous mine shafts. Lots of signs telling what went on and where, but they're not as gripping as reading someone's own words, like Gweniver's.

Caleb's holding my hand, and right now everything feels cool. I still haven't made sense of all that I've found out about my family. I know certain facts, like where I come from and that I have more relatives than I ever imagined, even in Cornwall, but it isn't as simple as that. Who I think I am now (did I ever know before?) seems to be tied up with Gweniver's and Redvers' story, but strangely enough, Caleb's too. And it's not just the knowing what happened to them, but their happiness, pain and loss has actually become part of me, as though I had to walk through their stories to find out my story is worth something too. There's more as well. A new picture is forming in my mind about being Australian that I have to come to terms with: that all Aussies weren't always fair, decent and sticking up for the underdog.

We climb the mound where the mine chimney is. Caleb bounds up ahead, grinning back at me. I like the way he walks; it's not a proud sort of confidence as if he owns the place but he walks lightly like he's a part of where he puts his feet. From up there we can see all the hills; everything green from the early winter rain. We stand there grinning at nothing, arms round each other's backs, me thinking about Caleb going north in the holidays to the camel races with his boss.

It makes me wonder if we see the same thing when we look at it, and I think we look too much at the differences. Gweniver's story has taught me there's enough the same. Hers is a story that will never end for it lives on in Dad and me, Kate and Hamilton, the Hayes family in Cornwall, and how many others?

From now on there'll be reminders everywhere. When we head back to the house, I see the white roses, ancient, but they don't look as straggly as I thought when we first came, more like rambling. Then there's the pepper tree that I now know my triple-great-grandmother planted. Every time we walk under it Caleb kisses me.

POSTLUDE

From: Royal Cornish Library
To: Jenefer Tremayne
Subject: Zenna Dare

Dear Jenefer

We have come across this article in the recent indexing of some of our newspapers and magazines and saw from our records you were researching Zenna Dare. Hope this is still useful.

Regards

Lisa Rowse

THE GENTLEMEN'S MAGAZINE

REFLECTIONS OF A THEATRE-GOER

October 1849

Whatever has happened to Miss Zenna Dare? All the world of theatre has been awaiting her next performance. Suddenly we are treated to a nightingale par excellence. The spontaneity of her singing was unaffected, ethereal, and for three seasons we were treated thus. But for a year now, there is no word of her performing again.

When questioned, Mr. Richard Drew makes no comment. In fact he is uncommonly tight-lipped about Miss Zenna Dare. He was Miss Dare's manager, and although it is said he enjoys the company of the fair sex, Miss

Dare's obvious integrity added interest to the professional relationship that theatre-goers observed. Indeed it seemed the perfect partnership. Behind stage they were dubbed the wolf and the lamb.

Miss Ginny Rivers has valiantly filled Miss Dare's roles and Mr. Drew has recently been seen in the Music Halls with a new protegee, a Miss Lilly Palmer. But Miss Palmer has not yet acquired a happy method of returning from her soaring falsettos. No other performance can compare to Miss Dare's impassioned performance in 'The Jewess' at Drury Lane last season. Prince Leopold could not marry a Jewess, even after he had fallen in love with her, and Miss Dare's farewell song, as the Jewess, before she jumped into the cauldron of oil, was so moving as to have dampened the eyes of all the company present.

Is it possible that this was truly a farewell to us all by the incomparable Miss Dare? Has she deserted us for holy matrimony or has she some fearful, debilitating disease? We all hope not. London has not tired of Miss Dare, a wistful and tender young lady who can melt hearts with a simple tune. She has been graced by God with talent and could well become this century's Queen of Song.

Please return to us, Miss Zenna Dare.

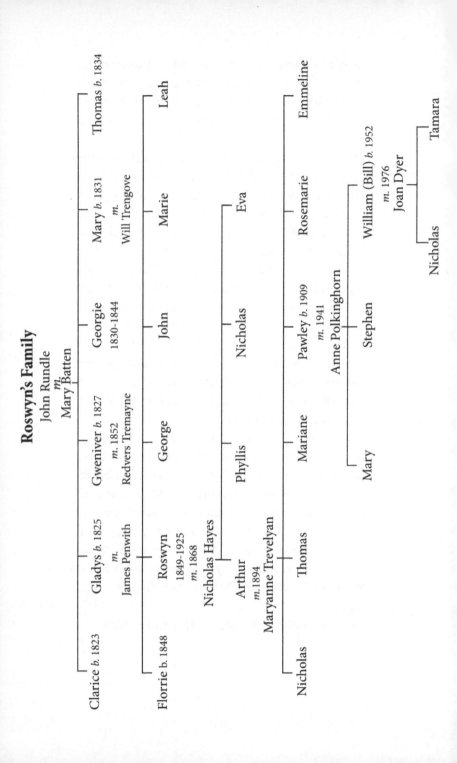

Roswyn's Family

John Rundle
m.
Mary Batten

Clarice *b.* 1823

Gladys *b.* 1825
m.
James Penwith

Gweniver *b.* 1827
m. 1852
Redvers Tremayne

Georgie
1830-1844

Mary *b.* 1831
m.
Will Trengove

Thomas *b.* 1834

Florrie *b.* 1848

Roswyn
1849-1925
m. 1868
Nicholas Hayes

George

John

Marie

Leah

Arthur
m. 1894
Maryanne Trevelyan

Phyllis

Nicholas

Eva

Nicholas

Thomas

Mariane

Pawley *b.* 1909
m. 1941
Anne Polkinghorn

Rosemarie

Emmeline

Mary

Stephen

William (Bill) *b.* 1952
m. 1976
Joan Dyer

Nicholas

Tamara

Gweniver's Family

Gweniver Rundle

m. 1852
Redvers Tremayne

Emmeline 1853-1894	Mary-Jayne 1854-1874	Percy 1855-1901	Nathan 1855-1912	Thomas 1857-1930	Rebekah 1859-1860	John 1860-1885	William 1862-1941	Elliot 1863-1923

Albert 1880
m. 1913
Honour Davies

Thomas 1857-1930
m. 1885
Rose Moyle

Nathan	Mary	James	George	Elizabeth

Dulcie	William	Dickie d. 1941	Dorie	Emily

William
m. 1945
Mary Rees

Maryann	Joy	Mark Tremayne

Maryann
m.
Paul Hart

Mark Tremayne
(I) *m.* 1980
Nicky Batten

Jenefer

(II) *m.* 1990
Steffanie O'Brien

Kate	Hamilton

Sources

Zenna Dare is a work of fiction. Although a handful of names are mentioned who did live in the mid-nineteenth century (Charles Hempel, Mrs Orchard, Dr Blood, Mr Buchanan, Jemmy Chambers, the Hawke brothers [my children's ancestors], and Richard Hawke [ancestor of Bob Hawke]), the characters in *Zenna Dare* bear no resemblance to any character living then or now. Nor is *Zenna Dare* based in any way on the life of the English actress, Zena Dare, born in 1887.

Jenefer's manse is consistent with other buildings built at the time and is based upon the Congregational Manse in Kapunda which is a heritage-listed building. The Bible Christian Manse was not like the manse depicted in this story and was in a different street.

Since this is a work of fiction the reader may find some dates have been changed; for example, *The Bohemian Girl's* opening night was in 1843 not 1846. Also, the poem by William Blake, 'The Sick Rose', has been included even though it might not have been known at the time Gweniver lived.

The poem Richard Drew dedicated to Zenna, inserting her name, is 'To Jane' by Percy Bysshe Shelley 1792–1822.

Descriptions of knockers can be found in Hunt, Robert, *The Drolls, traditions and superstitions of Old Cornwall*, 1881, Felinfach: Llanerch Publishers, 1993.

Information about the Ngadjuri people can be found in the work of Warrior, F, Knight, F, Anderson, S and Pring, *A Ngadjuri: Aboriginal people of the Mid North Region of South Australia:*, Meadows SA: SASOSE Council, 2005.

A playbill very much like the 'Sixpenny Entertainments' can be found in McCarthy, P, Krips, M and Turrell, I, eds, *Retrospect 1886*, Kapunda: Kapunda High School, 1986.

A ride north similar to Gweniver's in Jemmy Chambers' mail cart with a broken pole can be found in Kerr, M G, *Colonial Dynasty: Chambers family of SA*, 1980.

Many old tales about old Kapunda can be found in *Memories of Kapunda and District*, A Circle of Friends, 1929.

The full inscription on Joseph Emidy's grave can be found in the prologue of McGrady, R, *Music and Musicians in early nineteenth century Cornwall: the world of Joseph Emidy — slave, violinist and composer*, Exeter: University of Exeter Press, 1991.

Descriptions of Camborne where Gweniver grew up can be found in Thomas, C, *Christian Antiquities of Camborne*. Warne, HE,1967.

Descriptions of Gwennap where Redvers grew up can be found in James, CC, *A History of Gwennap*.